When Being Left is Right

Kirsten Leggett and Katerina Vangelis

Copyright © 2019

All rights reserved. This book or any portion thereof may not be reproduced or used in any manner whatsoever without the express written permission of the author except for the use of brief quotations in a book review.

Printed in Australia
First Printing, 2019
ISBN: 978-0-6484641-3-6

For our teachers...

In all their forms

Contents

Acknowledgements i

Foreword iii

Introduction 1

The Point of No Return 9

Overflow 17

A Cry for Freedom 25

The Wounding 43

Illusouly 59

Scraping it off Bones 67

Himalaya Calls 85

Surrender 107

Separation 127

Just for the Record 137

Sister Maria 159

Search and Rescue 165

Pink Ted 169

Transformation 183

Full Circle 193

Bibliography 208

Acknowledgements

The weaving of our stories has been many years in the making, and has required time away, solitude and multiple journeys into wild spaces, in both our inner and outer worlds. For this, we thank our partners in life, Chris Geale and Peter Leggett, for understanding our need to connect, discuss and dissect, explore and resolve, but most importantly, the space in which to embrace a new and loving friendship. To our children, in all your ages and stages of life, we thank you for listening and understanding our need to share our story. It means the world to us.

We extend our thanks to Maggie Kudelka and Alison Bleyerveen for your professionalism, your time and attention to detail, and your guidance in the delivery. To our friends and extended families, who have listened, enquired and encouraged us every step of the way with your enthusiasm and unwavering support.

To Robert Moss, our fabulous mentor and teacher on all things dreaming. We first discovered your work during the writing of this book, and your insightful words provided confirmation over and over on the significance of our dreams, providing us with so many "Aha" moments along the way. We cannot thank you enough for your generosity and kindness in writing the Foreword and introducing our story so eloquently.

Our thanks would not be complete without acknowledging all mothers and children and the ways in which our story connects with the mother-child relationship universally. To witness mothering in all its forms is such a gift.

We are filled to the brim with gratitude and the brightest of blessings.

Foreword

When Being Left is Right is a beautiful, courageous and deeply moving narrative of a soul friendship. Two women with complementary life experiences - as a daughter who was abandoned by her mother when very young, and as a mother, compelled by a life calling to leave her own children when they were young - come together to heal and be healed. We learn how trauma is held in the body and how healing becomes available as it is released and expressed. We see all the good that comes when we exercise the power to forgive ourselves and others.

We are made vividly aware of how dreams are not only the language of soul, but lay paths for us to reclaim lost soul and grow towards a greater Self. This book may bring tears to your eyes, but you will find that tears of empathy and recognition soon become tears of joy. May you be blessed to find a friendship as deep and creative as that of Kirsten and Katerina. You will be awakened by their story to recognize how the passions of the soul can work magic. You may find yourself inspired to write your own Book of Life and turn histories of pain and loss into a bigger and braver story.

- Robert Moss, author of *Conscious Dreaming, Dreaming the Soul Back Home* and *The Boy Who Died and Came Back.*

Introduction

When Being Left is Right combines two very personal stories on how life experiences, both pleasant and otherwise, can influence the way we move and respond to situations in our world. It is a rich and layered story, and when peeled back to the core, reflects how essential it is that we honour ALL of our life experiences, especially those that are deeply traumatic and wounding, for they can provide the gateway to astounding emotional and spiritual healing.

This story is written by two women who inadvertently meet each other under everyday circumstances, but connect on a much deeper level, as they begin to unravel their stories in each other's company. It is a story that presents both sides of the coin, one relating to a mother who chose to leave her young children, and the other a child who was abandoned by her mother at the age of four. It is here, at this junction where shame and guilt collide with the crippling fear of rejection and loss, that a storm of emotions erupts and cuts to the core of all that matters – deep and unwavering maternal love. In turn, they become the mirror for each other's stories, and together join hands and hearts to heal.

Many mothers could not bear the thought of ever leaving their children, but perhaps there are many who have come close to doing so or wished that they could have under certain circumstances. For the most part, these mothers may not feel able to express this thought, largely due to social conditioning and a quick to judge attitude about what mothers should and shouldn't do. This is not a story that encourages one way or another, nor is it a story of judgement, but is one that explores and pulls apart the seams that holds this notion together, diving beneath the surface and exposing the challenges one might endure when trying to live a life upholding their truth.

Many children in our world have been left at some point in their young lives, and the reasons why a parent chooses to leave is not well explained at the time, or the child is considered 'too young to understand.' There is always a need for the child to understand, whether it be at four, ten, thirty or well into the elder years. The child is forever within us and has far more wisdom than we give him or her credit for. If we listen to the child within, we expand our understanding of who we really are and find an inner joy in ways we never thought possible. We can reach a point in our lives when we give thanks for our life experiences and live out our days in shining authenticity.
We can all return home – in time, and with love.

Katerina

As a small infant I remember waking up feeling happy to a beautiful face above me with warm, velvety eyes. I felt welcomed with the sounds of soft cooing and a melodic voice radiantly smiling over me. I was encased in love - by my mother. She was my entire world.

At the time of birth and after the struggle of emerging into the physical world, we are placed on our mother's belly. Every cell of our tiny body seeks nourishment. To suckle and physically bond with her and to be held securely in her loving embrace knowing she means safety, warmth and love. It is here in her arms that our basic needs are met. The bond of love that is felt in that powerful moment when mother and child first connect is like no other. It is something our body and soul does not forget.

An abandoned child, at any age, may experience the breaking of this bond as heartbreak, and be left longing for security and love that only a mother can give. I was once told that the cracks created by a broken heart allows space for the heart's capacity for love, to grow and expand. This has been my personal experience, as a mother who chose to leave her children. I can understand how one would be quick to judge, or hasty to say, "*How could someone do that to a child?*" Yet there are always two sides to a story. There are many reasons why a mother may choose to leave, but these are not often shared or discussed because of the guilt and shame attached to such an act. The decision however, is never an easy one. For decades I carried the guilt, clinging to my skin like a heavy cloak. I worked hard to understand, to make amends, to continuously reassure my children that they are loved. I convinced myself I had this particular baggage all sorted out. I had unpacked that case many times and come to terms with all that was done. I had it covered, or so I thought until the day I met Kirsten and her inner four-year-old abandoned child.

Through her eyes and heart, I witnessed the many ways in which leaving a child can cause deep emotional trauma, and the need for the child within the adult to understand. Children do not 'get over it' quickly even though this may seem the case to the adult looking on. They carry the pain for many years, decades, and perhaps their entire lifetime unless they are given permission to speak their truth - to give a voice to all that has been held within but not fully understood.

The path I travelled has been of my own volition, influenced by choice and a deep conviction that I must live my life in a way that brings peace to all aspects of myself - body, mind and soul. There have been sacrifices along the way, heart wrenching decisions that have ripped me in two, and of course the unintentional consequences of my actions left in the wake. The guilt I carried for decades was revived the day Kirsten unravelled in my presence. Her entrance through my door and into my life was by no coincidence. I have learnt much from her inner child and together we have heard each other's truth and we have touched each other's pain to come to a new level of understanding. I can say, we have moved mountains. Extraordinarily, we have uncovered more than what lay beneath the surface of our skins - a story long forgotten but rekindled as soul connections are realised and past life patterns align. With each other's help, and unconditional love, we have come full circle.

Kirsten

Looking back, I see my childhood and experiences of abandonment as a gift, and that without this seemingly unfortunate start in life, I would not be in the position to see all that has unfolded as the most beautiful journey – in finding myself and the love that lies within. The wounding of the past has opened me up in ways I would never have thought possible, and by being a willing participant in this process, I have gathered pieces of my fractured self and brought them home. I have at long last shown myself great love.

For so long my inner child longed to experience all that she had missed out on, the love from a mother. As I grew into my adult years, that seed of longing also grew until a small crack in my heart allowed it to surface and be exposed at the age of forty-three. It was grief that would show me the way. I needed to return to my childhood, and to experience that which I had longed for, to see life through the eyes of a child once again, and to touch all that I had missed. It is only through this process that I have met my adult self with a new understanding and truly embraced who I am, knowing that all the love I need is within me. This is the light that has shown me the way home. I could not have done this without the love and understanding of Katerina, my spirit mother, teacher and soul friend – my *Anam Cara*[i]. It may have been the mirroring of events that drew us closer, but it was the surfacing of old attachments that provided the greatest learning and the deepest healing. The attachments to longing, guilt, abandonment, self-doubt, despair - to name just a few. Together we read each other's stories and as each page was turned, we reached a new understanding through the eyes and heart of each other.

Katerina's patience and willingness to stand by my side and encourage me every step of the way has been the most magnificent gift, and the most beautiful demonstration of compassion and understanding of one's need to find their way - the path to who they really are and who they wish to be. Through this journey of truth, I have uncovered much, and continue to do so every day, always open to the unexpected and the unexplainable, the long forgotten and the longed for. I have at last found the path to an inner freedom I never knew existed.

It is not uncommon for two people to come into each other's lives at exactly the time when they are needed the most. Whether one realises it at the time is neither here nor there, as the meaning of the connection and significance becomes apparent over time. How often do we hear "We were meant to meet each other on that day," or "I feel as though I have known her forever?" This is a life experience that many are familiar with, and it is an aspect of human relationship that we can relate to. Yet the story within this book describes a connection between two people that perhaps is not so commonly recognised, for it not only spans decades but reaches across time, as we discovered our deep connection in other lives lived, through our dreams. In fact, our story would make a great work of fiction, except that every word of it is true, every memory is real, and every dream validated. For two people in this world, in this moment in time, *being left is right* and it was right to leave in so many ways.

The Point of No Return

It was June 2011, a cold, wet and wintery day, and I had a new client scheduled in for the afternoon. I remember this day so clearly and is a day I will never forget. At this point in time, I had been practicing as a remedial massage therapist and Bowen therapy practitioner for 25 years. I found Bowen therapy to be a gentle, safe and unobtrusive modality in helping the recipient find balance in body, mind and soul. I loved my practice and found it highly rewarding, meeting and helping people from all walks of life. When I opened my door to a new client, I would never know what hidden gems were waiting to be discovered.

On this particular afternoon, I opened the door to meet Kirsten and immediately noted her petite and elf-like facial features, innocent green eyes and sandy coloured straight hair that softly framed her face. Immediately I felt her warmth and sensitivity, but intuitively detected an underlying fear. On the surface she seemed open, inviting and articulate as I questioned her on her medical history. She presented with carpel-tunnel syndrome including a restriction in a range of movement associated with her neck and shoulder, but the most painful of all was her sciatic discomfort. As she lay prone on the table, intuitively I sensed she was holding onto grief, but I said nothing about this at the time. She also seemed utterly exhausted as she lay on the table. Quietly I commenced her treatment; no more needed to be said.

Kirsten's treatments continued over the next few weeks as her body responded well, and her symptoms were abating, although the feeling of an underlying grief, which I detected during her first session, was still present in her body. As we talked some more throughout this session I learned that Kirsten had been devoting much of her time nurturing her best friend Vanessa, who was dying from a rare type of bone marrow cancer called myelofibrosis. The stress was taking its toll on Kirsten physically, mentally and emotionally, and this was not surprising as they had known each other for many years and had a strong, sisterly relationship. It was clear to me that Kirsten's heart was despairing at the thought of losing her closest friend, which she knew would come, and inevitably around Christmas that same year, Vanessa sadly passed away.

I had not seen Kirsten for four months, when she called to make another appointment. Her grief was palpable from the moment she walked through my door, and although I was aware of her recent loss, her grief seemed so much older than the recent grief of losing her dear friend. I could sense that something incredibly heavy was weighing on her. I had no idea what this was at that time, but upon reflection, I could see that Vanessa's passing had connected with something much deeper. It had been awakened, now simmering just below the surface.

During the session as we talked about how Kirsten was physically feeling and processing her friend's death emotionally, our conversation suddenly changed course, Kirsten began talking about a recent realisation around the losses of significant women in her life; a realisation she had received in a dream. She spoke of her most recent loss with the passing of Vanessa, she spoke of her much-loved grandmother, and then a brief mention of her mother. I could hear a slight trembling in her voice as she mentioned the word "Mother." I was intrigued by this and so I gently enquired some more. "Tell me more about your mother?" Without any more prompting her words tumbled out with such urgency, "My mother left me when I was four." There, right there, that was the defining moment, the first instance when the fissure in Kirsten's heart was revealed, and I first glimpsed the tiny four-year-old behind her eyes. With these words, an image cut through me so sharply and hit a cord so deep within my own heart, which took me completely by surprise. "Gently, gently" my inner voice guided me, "Just listen, observe," and so I did.

As I sat in the room with Kirsten and listened intently to her quiet words, I felt a subtle shift in her energy and within seconds the floodgates opened, tears cascaded down her cheeks and the raw wound within her heart was revealed as she crumbled before my eyes. All this time she had held onto so much sadness, confusion and fear, and my permission to allow her to speak about this traumatic event in her life was overwhelming - that I could see. The rawness of her recent loss combined with her childhood trauma had ripped the fissure wide open, shaking her foundations to the core. Clearly, this was the first time someone had been there for her, to listen attentively to her story.

In this moment our stories connected, my own undertow of emotion arrived, pulling and wrenching my heart in so fast, it felt as though it was churning and tumbling through a time machine. A torrent of emotions was surfacing for me also, flapping like a fish out of water gasping for air. It took every ounce of my being to prevent my own emotions from being expressed, and as a professional practitioner, I knew I had reached a line I could not morally cross. I remained so still and quiet waiting for the next sound, the next strand of her story, trying as best as I could to remain attentive and alert. However, despite my best intentions, I barely heard a word Kirsten was saying as my own heart felt as though it was being ripped from my centre. All I could remember were the first eight words blurted out at the beginning of our session, "My mother left me when I was four," and the unexpected ripple effect of Vanessa's passing, as Kirsten connected with her grief, and I with mine.

She was oblivious of course to the reactions occurring within me, as I in turn, tried to come to grips with the impact the inner four-year-old within Kirsten was having on me, for I could not ignore the fact that I too am a mother who abandoned her three children. I first left them at home with their father while I went on my first ever independent holiday, travelling and backpacking with a friend, and when I returned I was far from the same person. Through circumstances beyond my control I had no other choice but to leave permanently. The ages of my children at the time were ten, four and barely two. My session with Kirsten was the first time in my life I had the opportunity to glimpse into their world, suddenly finding myself at the front line and bearing witness to an abandoned child, listening to the pain in her heart and sensing her longing for a mother's love. Through Kirsten, I saw my own children and couldn't help but wonder that the pain she endured for all these years was a mirror for them also.

It was apparent that for the first time in her life Kirsten was given permission to speak about her trauma from a four-year old's perspective. She had not been given this opportunity until now and ironically, I was the person she had chosen to share this with. Within time Kirsten settled and was able to compose herself enough to continue talking, yet ever so softly. I felt like a traitor somehow, standing there in the room listening to her story of abandonment, while recognising my role in a parallel situation. I desperately wanted to tell Kirsten of my dilemma, but I was fully aware that I would cross a professional boundary, and perhaps risk the loss of a client who I would dearly love to work with.

So, I continued over many sessions to support the space for Kirsten to purge her pain and listen to the small inner four-year-old and her trembling voice, so soft and timid that I could barely hear her at times. As I increased my concentration tenfold, she took me back in time with her, revisiting an old place that she had not been to for so long, one filled with intense loneliness and sadness. Her fear and resistance at being here was overwhelming and trying to find the words to express herself was like trying to extract teeth. I could see how difficult it was for her. I spoke gently, to ease her fear and to reassure her that she was safe to express herself and to give voice to the story that lay in her heart. At times her emotions were so intense she struggled to breathe, turning her face to the right and tucking her chin into her shoulder, with her left hand attempting to hide her face. I could see there was so much fear around expressing her truth, and it was clear to me that this was how she protected herself, by saying nothing, guarding her inner four-year-old from the unbearable pain. It was excruciating for me to watch from the sidelines, but from a professional standpoint I needed to remain detached and fully present. I asked myself time and time again, "What, or who was she so afraid of?"

I would never have imagined such a moment, a wormhole in the universe of time fusing our stories together. I did not realise the significance of it then, but this was the beginning of what has become a treasured relationship, giving us both the opportunity to heal old and deep wounds, that I myself was in denial of, up until that moment. Kirsten became my abandoned child, and the guilt and shame that burdened my heart revealed itself, like ill-fitting shoes that made my whole body feel uncomfortable. Yet these were shoes I couldn't take off and replace with something else, because on some level, I felt I deserved the pain.

I had to walk this path, and at this point I knew there was no turning back for either of us.

Overflow

When you opened this door
I had no idea how deep the room was
How dark the cupboard
With its hundred-fold drawers
And endless memories

How easy it is to open one again
To see the skeleton
Held by a wisp of fear
A tenuous thread
To the longing

Kirsten Leggett

I remember a question that Katerina asked me during one of my early consultations, as it took me completely by surprise. "Are you grieving for anyone?"

I was taken aback by this question, as I tried to connect the dots between my aching hip and loss. The only response I could think of was relating to my closest friend Vanessa, and her death that would inevitably come, in the following months or even years. No one really knew when this moment would be, and I was secretly hoping it would be a long time yet into the future. I shared these thoughts with Katerina.

"No," she replied. "I don't think that's it."

We put the subject to rest and continued with my treatment. This was my first experience of Bowen Therapy and now I was even more intrigued by this approach in treating and healing physical ailments. This was not a line of questioning I was familiar with and it made me feel a little unsure, somewhat cautious and protective at feeling exposed.

The weeks passed, and I was relieved to be making good progress. My body was starting to feel so much better and after my third session I was astounded at the energy levels I had. I felt the best I had in years, so I continued with this therapy every six weeks or so as it was definitely making a difference, and everything about it felt so right for me. Within twelve months of my treatment and seeing Katerina regularly, Vanessa was admitted into palliative care, and so I shuffled and reprioritised my commitments to do all that I could for her. She had recently divorced, so I helped where I could by bringing her children in to see her in the morning, dropping them back to school, heading back to work, collecting my own children, then working from home to make up for lost time. I was incredibly busy, but I was convinced I would manage, for I had no idea how much time we had left or how many more conversations we would have together. It was worth every early morning and every late night, for I could always pick up the pieces afterwards; and so, this lifestyle continued as we slid into the end of the school year and into the chaotic pace of Christmas.

Vanessa was so determined to spend Christmas Day with her children. She knew it would be her last and so we set about making it the most memorable Christmas ever. Every wish her children had that year was granted, and it gave me such joy to find her the little things to fill their stockings and bring bigger smiles to their faces. We talked late afternoon on Christmas Day, and I listened as she cried over the phone at how happy her children were, how they had told her it was the best Christmas they had ever had. I silently cried too on the other end of the line, knowing how hard it was for her just to get this far, to hold onto life for this moment to spend her last Christmas with her children. Her grit and determination were unwavering and like no other I had seen.

We finished our conversation that Christmas Day and I told her I would see her in the morning, come and give her a big hug and bring her morning coffee, as I had done ever since she entered palliative care six weeks earlier. It was a ritual we had established during this time, and it was as though life was normal in these moments, distracting us from the reality that was. Here, we were like any two friends talking over coffee and life felt normal.

On Boxing Day as I was on my way to see her, coffee in hand, I received a call from her brother. Vanessa had passed away early that morning around 6am. Even though I knew this news would come one day, it was still like hearing a conversation in a foreign language. It never quite sunk in, as though some impermeable barrier was keeping it at bay. All I could think of was that it couldn't be true, I had just heard her voice the night before, and now I would never see her again or sit and talk as we had done on so many mornings. That day instead was a day where I would sit with her children as they were told their mother had passed away, it was the day where I would hold them as they cried and cried in disbelief that they would never see her again, never be held by her, just one more time, never another Christmas like they had just had. In some way, I knew how they were feeling. My mother did not die of course, but the sudden absence and realisation that she was gone, was something my body remembered well, and it made me feel sick to the stomach. My heart was wedged in my throat all day, but I managed to hold it together for her children and for mine, for if I let it out I didn't know whether I would be able to stop it. From the inside, everything was heaving against the seams.

The days and weeks that followed passed by in a blur, as I experienced the impact of Vanessa's sudden absence in my life and the gaping hole she left. Several months had passed when I felt my body needed attention as every part of me ached, so I scheduled another session with Katerina. The moment I walked through her door I could see that she sensed something was amiss, and just as much as I wanted to get on with the treatment and put my grief aside for the next hour, she seemed to know that there were words I needed to say, and a well of emotion I was holding in. Vanessa's death was still raw and although I had stepped back into life as it was, it was not the same without her. We were close, like sisters, and it felt as though part of me was missing. I had never felt lonelier. As I began to talk about my loss and Vanessa's passing, tears flowed, and I wiped them away, embarrassed that I could no longer hold them in. I cried and talked and received a gentle treatment that afternoon. All I wanted to do was to retreat inward and settle into the quietness of the session. Looking back at this time with Katerina, I realise it was indeed, the calm before the storm.

I continued to see Katerina every four to six weeks depending on how my body was feeling and responding to treatment. I was working my way through grief and I was feeling more open to talking about how I was feeling and processing things. Katerina was wonderfully gentle with me during this time, and it felt good to talk about death and grief so openly; to walk away from these sessions with greater insight, knowing that what I was feeling was perfectly normal. I was dreaming more and more too, with such great clarity and it felt good to talk to someone about my dreams, especially someone who seemed to understand exactly why I was dreaming this way, and the messages they were bringing me. She helped me navigate this rocky period as though she knew every step and every feeling grief could throw my way. She was able to provide a level of insight to my dreams that I understood and made me feel safe, to unravel.

Unravel I did one day, in the midst of winter, in the most spectacular way. I arrived at my morning appointment feeling so sad and deflated, and I was struggling to simply be in the world. I felt beaten to a pulp on the inside. We always talked a little before we started the session, and on this occasion, I mentioned to Katerina something significant I had both felt and seen one night, in that moment between wakefulness and sleep – a dream or vision of sorts. I told her of the layers of grief I could both feel and see lying within me, and the realisation that somehow, they were all linked, that one layer was the opening to the next, and that layer to yet another. I explained further, speaking of my grief for Vanessa, then the passing of my grandmother, and then finally the loss of my mother at the age of four. It was the mention of the mother layer that caused my voice to waver slightly, and so I quickly recovered and moved on, changed the subject. Case closed. It was not important, it was history. I had long since dealt with that and did not see the reason why I should elaborate on this part of my life any further.

However, I did not anticipate the enquiry that would follow, and the emotion in my voice that piqued her curiosity; then her words "Let's go back to your mother for a minute, tell me more about her." In that single moment it was as though the floodgates had been opened, I could not hold it back anymore, the dam was bursting; my seams splitting and it all came spewing out, gushing over the edge, as I crumbled into a thousand pieces and sobbed my heart out. I don't remember a word of what I said, only that the sadness I had held onto for forty years squeezed its way through the cracks, wound its way up my throat and hurtled out of my mouth at great speed, as if for the very first time. It was like a raging torrent I could not stop. There was no thought, just the words of a frightened and confused four-year-old, struggling to make sense of it all and finally having permission to express what lay in her heart.

I had reached the point of no return and my mind was spinning. As a child, I could never recall any adult asking me how I was feeling, how I was coping, did I need to talk? Instead it felt as though everything was swept under the mat, sent into hiding for it was too hard to face, and perhaps too difficult to find the answers for - too difficult to console an inconsolable child. So, it was here I first witnessed my fractured self, in the safety of a small room with a woman I had known for little more than a year – baring my soul. I still recall the look of shock on her face as she watched me from a distance, listening to the words that seemed to have no ending and no structure. Words lost amongst the tears, and a sadness which filled the room. When there were no words left, only tears, Katerina asked me, "Did she ever come back?" I shook my head. "Not when I needed her."

I felt completely shattered after this session, and embarrassed that I had such a monumental melt-down in front of a virtual stranger. What would she think? Had I said too much? Would she ever want to see me again? Was I an emotional basket case? I wanted to erase the past hour and press restart. I felt ashamed and embarrassed by my emotional outburst, but I felt so relieved when she asked me to come back for another appointment. Surely, I could make amends for my lack of self-control. Then, as I was about to turn and walk out her door, both exhausted and in shock from all that had unfolded, she asked me for something I was least expecting – a hug. Like a magnet I fell into her arms and she held me so tight. I drew back a little for I did not normally allow such closeness, but she pulled me closer still, and it was then that I felt the most beautiful energy pass through me like a gentle breeze. I lingered in that space for a little while and felt the word "beautiful" resonate throughout my whole mind and body. As though she knew what I was thinking, Katerina whispered quietly, "Oh, you *ARE* beautiful."

In that single moment in time, I connected with something so much bigger than me, so much stronger than anything I had ever encountered in my life thus far. It enveloped and held me with such tenderness. It was like reaching into a dark corner of the cupboard and finding something that I had long forgotten and long given up on. I did not know it then, but it was the very thing my heart had longed for, all this time.

It was motherly love.

A Cry for Freedom

*"Freedom is not about the size of your cage
or power of your wings or non-attachment
to a person or thing.*

*Freedom is about being so truly, madly and deeply
attached to your own soul that you can't bear –
if only for a moment –
a life that doesn't honour it."*

Andrea Balt

There was a time, where I couldn't help but feel slightly uncomfortable when I saw Kirsten's name in my weekly appointment schedule. I wanted to help her in every way possible, but with each visit she left me feeling more and more vulnerable to the memories of my own story. Her extreme difficulty in speaking her truth and finding her voice, was one that was deeply personal for me also, one that I had struggled with for much of my life. I could see that Kirsten's trauma as a child had frozen her in such a way that she did not feel safe to voice what lay in her heart. She had grown conditioned to protect herself, but by doing so had shut off her heart to the world. In my room, she was beginning to surface, ever so slowly, and somehow, I sensed she would be committed to the inner work to reclaim all that she had lost.

I too had experienced a similar awakening in my life, influenced by an upbringing that was stifled by culture and expectation. Like Kirsten, decisions were made for me that had long-lasting impacts and shaped the course of events in my life. This not only paralysed my confidence but took away any feelings of self-worth I may have gained by being able to make decisions for myself, on my own terms.

On reflection, I am grateful for these events and circumstances, for they have shaped and influenced my understanding of who I am, and who I have always strived to be. Our trials in life and the decisions we make along the way, or those that are thrust upon us, can provide us with opportunities for great learning, and, if we're open to it, deep healing. I knew this could be possible for Kirsten, and I was prepared to do anything I could to help her through her four-year-old trauma and retrieve a part of her soul that was lost.

Over many years I experienced personally and witnessed in my clients, aspects of soul retrieval. These experiences were not necessarily dramatic or filled with intense emotion, but most often involved a feeling of connection with something lost; a realisation that a part of the self was missing, and a sublime feeling of wholeness when that fragment of our self, of our soul, was welcomed home. Many aspects of our soul may be missing at different times of our lives, depending on our own sensitivities and the life experiences that may have caused us trauma.

I have always had an awareness of a deep connection with Soul, not only my soul, but a Universal Soul. I recall my own story, one that begins at a young age, when my inner soul yearnings stirred as I imagined myself travelling and exploring the world. While it may have taken me many years to achieve this, it is not surprising that the experiences that followed led to a profound awakening in my adult life. At seven years of age my fondest memory was playing with my cousins and sitting them down in front of my blackboard to teach them everything I had learnt at school that day. At that young age, teachers were my champions, and by the time I reached twelve, I realised that teaching was my calling. I told my parents that this was going to be my vocation, to travel the world for humanitarian causes and teach less advantaged children, for them to gain a better life. That was my dream, at least when I was twelve, but unfortunately that dream was never realised, for my parents had other plans in mind for me and my future.

I spent most of my teenage years' day dreaming; imagining a life of my choosing. In my daydreams I would travel to all four corners of the earth with my camera, capturing images of beautiful scenery, and foreign faces with life's experience engraved into every wrinkle. I would imagine people's facial expressions, as I took time to observe and be still – to discern life from every angle. This was the life I dreamt of, but I could never explain this in a way that my parents would understand, as it was a world so incongruent to the one they had based their own lives on, working hard to support a growing family. As such, it was their expectation that I would share a similar existence. It was the way in a fervently Greek household.

We were a poor family, always living on the edge of survival it seemed. My parents came from a tiny Greek island in the Aegean Sea, called Lipsi. It is one of twelve islets situated near the coast of Turkey, dotted like stepping stones across the Southern Aegean Sea. The island chain begins with Samos (home of Pythagoras) and ends with Rhodes, the ancient gateway to the Greek civilisation. During World War II these islands were decimated and occupied by the German and Italian forces. The local people suffered immensely, largely through starvation and suppression of their culture, and witnessed many atrocities including bombing of the main islands, the loss of critical infrastructure, and the death of friends and loved ones.

During war time my father was a seafarer, and because of his knowledge and navigation skills he was coerced by the German's to deliver supplies and to gain information into the locations of the surrounding islands for their own strategic purposes. From the outside it would be easy to view him as a traitor, but he was not a traitor to his people, for at the same time he was collaborating with the local community to map out an escape route to safety and a chance for their survival. His plan was to take them on his schooner to Palestine and live as refugees until it was safe enough to return home, but this plan would need to be executed at the right time, in the right moment and with great precision. Nothing could be left to chance. Through these acts of bravery, my father was considered a local hero by the community. He had already saved many lives and they considered him their "Captain," steering them towards ultimate freedom.

When the war ended, the people of Lipsi were left with the aftermath, the desolation of farms and vineyards that was once their livelihood. They were faced with the inevitable task of picking up the pieces and rebuilding their lives. This seemed impossible given the level of destruction and state of economic ruin. Hence, thousands of people immigrated to other countries in search of a better life. My father chose to relocate to Australia and arrived in this country three years ahead of my mother and two brothers, to prepare a new home and life for them. They were proud, handsome people with a heritage extending back thousands of years, and I was born into this family, in this new and lucky country.

Who was I to come along and dare to be different? To turn my back on the Greek Orthodox religion and traditions, a culture so enmeshed in community and family values, and where nothing else was more important. These values and principles formed a code for their lives that worked and was not to be trifled with, interfered with or questioned. It worked for them, but it certainly did not work for me. Where did this yearning come from? Why wasn't I happy being like everyone else? I questioned these thoughts regularly as I felt miserable but knew there was no place to seek solace from these feelings in my family home. As a child, I was happiest in the bedroom I shared with my younger sister. I would often order her out of the room so I could be alone in my secret world and find imaginative ways to escape my reality. Otherwise I considered my life awfully mundane and boring.

Between the ages of seven to twelve my existence revolved around school, church, housework and family, always being conditioned to meet the needs of my older brothers. In this culture it was a girl's obligation, despite her age. The rules of our household were firm, there was no socialising with other children who weren't part of the Greek community, especially Australians, for the fear of our culture being adulterated by the freedom the Australian life seemed to express. We weren't allowed to speak English at home or bring friends home after school. We were not allowed to play sport or participate with school sport on weekends. As a child I thought, "If only I could have a piano, at least some of the boredom would be alleviated if I could learn to play an instrument". There was a music shop across the road from where I lived, and I would pass by it each day after school. I would meander across the street to look at their window display of pianos, keyboards and guitars, and they offered lessons too. I longed for this to be my reality, but this wish was never granted.

Until the age of seven, life for me was generally joyful and I only recall hearing my parents raising their voices occasionally. I do remember my mother crying a lot and trying to think of ways to please her and make her happy. Songs from Greece would pour out of her in soft, dulcet tones yet they only seemed to make her more miserable. As I matured, my parents argued more. It was always over money, paying the bills and putting food on the table. Somehow there was never enough to stretch the distance.

I recall one night I was woken by my dad coming home and he stood at the door of the bedroom my sister and I shared with our parents. He called out for attention, and as my mother roused from her sleep he began pulling out wads of money from every pocket in his suit. Thousands of notes, it seemed never-ending. My brothers stumbled sleepily into the bedroom to see what the commotion was all about and watched as dad threw the money on to the bed. He shared it around, giving the boys fifty pounds each! He organised the rest into bundles, but my mother was not impressed and told him to take it away, uttering that it would be gone by tomorrow. He pleaded with her, "I got lucky tonight, a big win on the horses. All our financial worries are over!" My mother did not show an ounce of enthusiasm, there was only a blank expression on her face. Oblivious to her words he continued dividing the money, "This is for our bills, and this is for our house." At the mention of a house, he immediately got mum's attention. Her eyes lit up in hope and I could see that she believed him, that indeed there was a possibility that they would own their own home. Everyone was so joyful and happy.

At the time, I didn't quite understand what the fuss was about, but I relished the joy of the moment as he handed all his winnings to mum. However, the joy was short-lived and the following night the arguing resumed. Dad was dressed up and ready to go out when he turned to mum and demanded she give him the money. Of course, she said "No!" but her stubbornness was no match for my father's determination. Poor mum, she had no choice but to surrender to his demands and hand over the money. He left the house and my mother was left crying – again. Hours passed until he returned home, yet this time the situation could not have been more different. There were no smiling faces, no joy, and the enthusiasm of the previous night had disappeared. No one uttered a word. My father's demands continued as he approached my brothers, demanding they return the money he had given them the night before. Of course, they obeyed, somewhat reluctantly.

On his way out the door he turned to my mother and asked her to be happy for him, to send him off with positive thoughts, but she could do nothing but remain sunken and unhappy. I witnessed this cycle throughout their married life. They worked so hard, and if mum had not been the squirrel she was with her money, she would never have had her beautiful, modest house that she managed to buy and pay off on her own, while rearing a young family of five children. She may as well have been on her own, and perhaps that could have been a better alternative, at least she would not have to put up with the emotional roller coaster ride she was on.

When I was twelve, my father bought a fish and chip shop with the intention to provide us with a better life and financial security. My heart sank, for I knew I would be forced to work in this shop day and night; there would be no school holidays, no time to study, just work. I don't know how I knew this, but even at this age my intuition was strong. I had no doubt this would be my reality, and so it was. I endured this existence throughout my high school years, from grade seven through to grade ten, followed by one year working full time in the shop, when I should have been attending higher education in grade eleven. It wasn't easy. I watched any promise of financial security vanish because my father's gambling habit became worse, and he lost the profits made by our hard work. We had the busiest fish and chip shop in town, but my mother still needed to work as a cook in an Italian restaurant until 5am in the morning to make ends meet. She endured so much hardship, but she would never leave my father for fear of bringing shame to our family name.

These events undoubtedly shaped my perception of Greek men. I believed they were all the same – controlling and gamblers. At the back of my mind I was worried that if I married a Greek man, I too would have the life my mother had, which was far from the life I dreamed of. Inevitably, as the years passed and I matured, I was steered in this direction as was the tradition in our culture. I was not the master at the helm. One day when I was sixteen, my mother announced that it was time for me to marry. My initial reaction was complete shock and I wanted to respond to her vehemently with "No, never!" However, at that age, I did not have the confidence to confront my mother. I listened as she told me that I had already been betrothed to a man who was seven years my senior, at a time when I was just eleven years old.

Sixteen! I couldn't believe it. I knew there was no way out of this situation and that my fate was sealed. Little did I know, that the man to whom I was betrothed had been working with our family in the shop during his spare time for the past four years, knowing all that time that we were destined to marry, whereas I had only ever thought of him as like another brother. I was overwhelmed by this news, but regardless my mother proceeded with arrangements for the engagement party. Her plan for my future was unfolding as my own dreams of becoming a teacher and travelling the world were diminishing by the minute. All I had left was a dream I could only yearn for.

So, engaged and with the ring on my finger, there came a huge discomfort that this was not what I wanted for my life. My fiancée decided that before we got married he would to take a trip to America to visit his brother, followed by a trip to Lipsi to catch up with his parents before he returned home to me, and we would be wed. During his absence, I became increasingly anxious at the thought of marrying this man; the thought of marriage in general. It all seemed too soon, and I questioned where the love was in this relationship.

In mum's wisdom, we children were given private tuition for an hour every Saturday in Greek language, where I learnt to read and write quite well. This was fortunate for me, for as the weeks progressed, I decided to write my fiancée a letter and post it to Lipsi, so that it would arrive ahead of him. I found the courage to tell him that I could not marry him; that I would always value him as a brother and he was a wonderful person, but I would not make him happy because I did not love him, and doubted our marriage would last. I made the suggestion, to find a nice Greek girl on Lipsi who would cherish him and share the life that he dreamt of. As I posted the letter I felt relieved that I had spoken my truth in expressing my feelings. For the first time in months I could breathe again.

Six weeks passed, and I was working in the shop and serving customers when my mother walked in ranting and raving in Greek asking, "What have you done, what have you done?" I finished serving and calmly asked her to quieten down and that I would talk to her in the back room shortly. When I walked in she demanded to know why my fiancée had returned from Greece, inconsolable with a letter in hand that I had sent to him. I explained to her that if I went ahead with this marriage it would be over in a year, which in my mind would be far worse than breaking it off now. She demanded my father to talk to me about it, which he did, approaching the situation gently and softly, which surprised me. He asked me if I loved my fiancée, and I replied "No." He quietly responded, "That's okay, you don't have to do this."

My sense of relief was immediate but short lived, as the next two years was punctuated with meeting after meeting of prospective husbands. They rolled through our house one after the other as invited dinner guests. When they left, my parents would wait for my answer. It was always "No!" In my eyes, all these men were looking for was someone who could work in their shops and be a slave to their expectations. Most importantly, love was not a part of the equation. This was definitely not the life I wanted, but despite my protest, my parents were relentless in their task. There must have been at least fifteen men invited to our house over a two-year period. I was now eighteen, and my parents were determined to find me a husband. My mother thought I would be left 'on the shelf' as I continually rejected the men of their choosing. After a while, their efforts eventually subsided, and everything relating to marriage and husbands seemed off the agenda.

Then one day, several months later, my father announced an invitation he had received from his employer for his baby's baptism, and our whole family was invited. I had no interest in going as I had never met these people, however my father was intent on me going. He accepted my refusal to go to the church for the ceremony, but insisted I attend the reception, and I reluctantly agreed. We were gathered in a small community hall one warm December evening, greeting the family and their baby, and were then seated at the tables allocated for us. The hosting family was a Greek family from Cyprus. My second eldest brother had married a Greek girl from Cyprus, and through her, I had come to realise that their culture was a little more liberated and open than ours.

Suddenly, the host family became quite excited and animated as a tall, handsome young man entered the hall. He had dark, deep set eyes and a shiny smile, and everyone applauded in delight at his arrival. I had never seen such a reaction before towards a person, and he was clearly loved and adored by all. He apologised for arriving late and explained to us that he needed to pick up a new battery for his camera. As the night continued, there was much eating and dancing, and gradually it came to be that this young radiant man and I sat together and started to engage in conversation. He spoke English well and had just come to Australia from Manchester in England, where he had been studying accountancy for the last three years. He was articulate, smartly dressed and I liked him.

      The following day, I answered a knock on our front door to find him standing there. I was surprised and thought to myself, "What does he want here?" and under pretence he asked if he could see my father. Dad invited him in to the formal lounge, and instructed me to bring coffee and refreshments, as is the custom in a Greek household. When I returned, dad got up and left the room, and I found myself alone with him again. It didn't take long for me to put two and two together. This was an arrangement. My heart sank, but nevertheless, I thought he was a decent man, so never let on that I knew what he was there for. Over the next few weeks he came and went with dad's permission, and we gradually got to know each other better. We were never allowed out together, but he was welcome to see me in my parent's home.

During the summer holidays I was invited to my cousin's family's shack for a week, and when I returned home on Saturday afternoon my mum was up to her neck in cooking.

When Being Left is Right   37

"What's going on?" I asked, and she replied, "Just go and have a shower and put a nice dress on."

"But why? Who is coming? What's the fuss about?"

She said, "You'll see, you'll see. Hurry up and stop wasting time, they'll be here soon."

I did as I was told, and when I was dressed and ready I asked again, "Who's coming?" and when I was told it was Dad's boss, his family and their youngest brother, the penny dropped. I knew that the imminent visit was to ask for my hand in marriage. This was how it was done.

The family arrived, and we all had a lovely time catching up, but then it was down to business. Up to thirty people were gathered in the formal lounge room and dad sat by the two of us. He turned to me and announced that the young man had asked for my hand in marriage. I knew in my heart that I had to say no, because yet again this was not the life I wanted. I replied with, "No, I'm sorry, I'm not ready for marriage yet." As I finished giving my answer, I looked around me to see how sad and deflated everyone looked and immediately I felt embarrassed and guilty, ashamed that somehow I had hurt so many people. The pressure to conform to their expectations escalated, and so reluctantly I caved in and said, "Alright, I'll do it, I will."

In the moment those six words were spoken, the future I was destined to live became clear. At the time, I thought I could try and influence the situation to suit my terms and approached my father to ask for a two-year grace period, arguing the point that we could use the time to get to know each other better and save some money for a new beginning. He immediately declined my request, for he felt that this would shame our family name and if it didn't work out, my reputation would be tarnished, and no Greek man would ever want to marry me.

Within three months we were married and had a big fat Greek wedding, however I was not provided with a house, as was the tradition. Not that my husband minded, he had confidence that we could provide for ourselves. Times were tough, and we had to work hard, but in time managed to save enough money to buy into a grocery shop that we opened seven days a week. Here I found myself again, living my life in a way I had tried so hard to escape from. I felt stifled, but by that stage our family was growing, having already welcomed our first child. We adored her, she was an absolute delight and gave us such joy.

Within two years we progressed from shop to supermarket status, opening our store seven days a week from 8am to 8pm. I was living my own worst nightmare, reinforced to me day after day, week after week; a constant reminder that this was not the life I wanted. We did well financially, built an architecturally designed house and invested wisely. Six years later our family grew again with the birth of our son, soon followed by our second daughter two years later. Life had taken its toll on me over the years, and even though I loved my children more than life itself, I felt frustrated, stifled, angry and resentful. I yearned for the life I had imagined at the age of twelve. My burgeoning frustration and resentment manifested in my body and I was constantly ill with sinusitis, allergies and sheer exhaustion.

It was not long after my son was born when I began to experience things of a spiritual nature; events in my life I couldn't easily explain. I became open in a way that seemed to unfold naturally and of its own accord, but was enhanced when I started practicing meditation, providing me the personal space I needed to step back and take stock of my life. I became dedicated to this practice and act of self-care, as it enabled me to feel a sense of serenity and lightness I had never previously known. During this time of deep introspection and enquiry, I knew my life was going to change and that this change was inevitable, as too would be the emotional rollercoaster ride I would embark on.

During this time of internal focus, I also experienced severe neck and back pain, because of my body being out of alignment from pregnancy. After searching for months for someone suitable to help me, my sister recommended an osteopath, who also practiced as a naturopath and remedial massage therapist. This felt right for me on an intuitive level, and within six weeks he had my back and neck issues under control, along with several allergies I had endured over the years. I felt as though I had been reborn. I thanked him so much and thought to myself, "This is what I would love to learn and be" – a body therapist who practiced in this way, like him. If I could help someone as much as he had helped me, then I would have a most rewarding and fulfilling life. I had a new and exciting goal and I was prepared to reach for it, seeking guidance from him to point me in the right direction. He provided all the support and guidance I needed, and when I received my massage certificate one year later, he employed me to work in his natural therapy centre. Everything seemed to fall into place. He was my mentor, as well as my employer, and I was so happy, probably for the first time in my life, in a career path of my choosing. By this time, I was also pregnant with my third child, and the ability to work as a massage therapist opened a whole new world for me. This practice aligned with my own spiritual beliefs and philosophies, and even though I was not earning a great living from it, I felt rich within myself.

I loved my husband, but I was never in love with him and felt that he never quite "got" me, but on reflection, I realise it was me who needed to "get" me so that I could live my life authentically. He was a good man and father, ten years my senior but very controlling, constantly needing to demonstrate that he knew better; that he knew what was best for me. He too carried his own childhood trauma and I could see he needed help, but I was too confused myself to help him in this way, at this point in time. It seemed that we lived and communicated like two squabbling children, one battle after another, relentlessly arguing. I felt as though I was always defending my new world; or my authentic world which was the one I longed to live in. Again, I found myself in an all too familiar place, of having someone else dictate what my life should be and how it should be lived.

Over time, he wore me down to the point where I felt I had no other option but to surrender and retreat into a place of hopelessness. All I could see in front of me was the death of my true self, and the person I really wanted to be, lacking the courage to confront him, and allowing what I really wanted in life to slip away, day by day. Again, I had lost control of my own life and I grieved and grieved for the future my heart and soul desired.

My grief for this life lingered for decades, as did Kirsten's grief from being abandoned by her mother, although she had been unaware of it, until someone else she loved suddenly left her world. She too had spent so long not being able to express her feelings about this impactful event in her life, one that she had no control over or could influence in any way. I could also see that her grief was more than beyond her immediate loss at four years of age, but extended to the loss of a relationship she could have had with a mother who had stayed and nurtured her throughout her childhood years.

As we met and talked together, Kirsten stirred in me my own loss of the possible future I may have had with my children had I chosen a different path, and so began my own inner questioning and turmoil. I knew there was more for me yet, and how on earth could I help Kirsten, when I was so implicated and linked to the core aspects of her story? All I knew was that our truth was emerging at an alarming rate and that eventually I would need to share with Kirsten my own story.

The Wounding

*"I consciously sit in the seat of disturbance
And watch it enter the room*

*I see it now
For the gift that it is
And the freedom
It carries in its hand.*

*It is my greatest teacher,
A lesson born from the pain
Of a heart once broken.*

*It is in fact, the glue
That puts me back together."*

Kirsten Leggett *(2016)* [ii]

My session with Katerina that cold winter's day set me on a path of deep reflection and inner enquiry. As I experienced loss again in my life, it seemed my body had discovered a part of me that so desperately wanted to be heard. My four-year-old voice that had gone into hiding for over forty years was peeking through the cracks that had been created by new loss, and ever so slowly, was finding its footing in the world. Loss and I came face-to-face in the battle ring once again in the comfort and safety of

Katerina's room. It became a fierce and unforgiving battle where we danced around each other like old friends. I had already watched Vanessa, my closest friend of twenty years dance with death. I had watched on from the sidelines as she endured a battle that lasted seven long years, and it was one I never thought she would lose. Looking back to this moment, I can see that Vanessa's passing opened a door to the most beautiful gift – to an emotional freedom I never knew could exist. Grief, in all its rawness, became the catalyst to my own personal archaeological dig and an expedition like no other, one in finding my true self. It was as though Vanessa's absence in my life tore open a part of me that had been protected from the world for the best part of forty years. This fissure was not so wide at first, but as grief settled in and made itself at home, the crack widened and deepened to let just a sliver of light in. Grief was the wedge that enabled deep wounds to open, expose themselves and eventually heal.

At the time I could never have imagined, even in my wildest dreams, the journey that was to unfold. Day by day, month by month, year after year, the layers peeled back one after the other to expose the deep emotional wounds caused by loss. The first layer was a thin veneer compared to what lay underneath in the deepest part of me. I could have turned my back on all of this, buried it and continued with life as I knew it, but something compelled me to dig deeper and deeper and once I started I couldn't stop, diving into the murkiness of all that has been and all that had been lost. It was as though I intuitively knew something was there to be found and like a dog with a bone, I kept digging and digging until I could grasp it in my teeth and wrap my tongue around it so that I could truly taste it. I knew that then and only then, would I understand. It was a time travelling experience like no other and inevitable, that to reach its source, I would eventually return to the emotional age of four when my heart was first broken.

I read once that heartbreak is unpreventable for all of us, in one way or another. David Whyte best describes it as the "natural outcome of caring for people and things over which we have no control, of holding in our affections those who inevitably move beyond our line of sight"[iii]. For me, it was my own mother who moved beyond my grasp, when she walked out the door of our home when I was just four years old, leaving me behind with my father, brother, and sister. Life for my mother had become too much to bear and so she left, to start anew.

Whilst my mother remained present in my life, it was in small doses and then through circumstances beyond my control, she moved further and further away until I saw her just once a year at Christmas. It became a long-distance relationship held together with the most tenuous of threads, expectation and obligation. I loved her, for she was my mother, and I missed her with all my heart. As I grew, the calendar on my wall became the marker of that love as each day was crossed off and I drew one step closer to seeing her again, fortnight by fortnight, month by month and then eventually year by year. It was my never-ending routine, the one thing that kept me going when her absence in my life became more than I could possibly hold on my own.

My paternal grandparents did all they could for us in the early years and supported my father in his sole parenting. He worked hard to provide us with all that we needed with a roof over our head and food on the table. It seemed he was gone from dawn until dusk, until he tucked us back into bed each night. My first few years of school were spent rising early so that my father could drop us off to have breakfast with my grandparents before he travelled to work. My grandmother would then walk us up the hill to school. She was always there at 3 O'clock in the afternoon as the school bell rang, standing outside the gate to walk us back home again. Some of my fondest childhood memories are those with her, as we baked in her kitchen after school, walked along the riverbank searching for 'treasures' and building rock gardens at the shack on the shores of the Great Lake. She called me her treasure and I felt like one when I was with her. We made a home in the rock garden for the mountain skinks and we would sit quietly and watch them come out to bask in the sun and take a nibble from the strawberry in my tiny hand. She showed me the wonder of nature and found the space in which to reach in and touch my heart. She was the grandest mother of all.

My father eventually remarried the year I turned eight. I recall that year as one of much adjustment. Not only did we move interstate for twelve months, far from my grandparents and my own mother, but we shared our home with a new stepmother. In that year we also welcomed a new baby brother into our home. While this was an exciting time for our family, no one could prepare me for the change that followed, and as the months extended into years the intense bond between a mother and child became apparent. Nothing could come between it, for it was filled with so much love and even though I was still so small, it felt as though there was no space left for a stepchild to squeeze into. Watching from the sidelines, I could see and feel all that I did not have within arm's reach. I wished to be shown just a fraction of that love, to receive just an ounce of the tenderness, to feel a tiny moment of belonging – to a mother.

The stepmother archetype is one we are all familiar with. Children have listened to this story throughout generations, where the idea of the 'wicked stepmother' is the norm and where stepchildren are destined to wear rags, sweep the cinders from the hearth and be treated with disdain. I did not wear rags for clothes, all my physical needs were met, but what I did miss out on is the unconditional day-to-day love from a mother. Someone whom I could wrap my arms around and melt into just because I needed to be close, someone whom I felt safe with, someone who loved me for just the way I was, someone who smiled at me when I walked in the door. I knew this was possible and real for I had seen it with my own eyes when I visited friends, stayed with cousins, and saw mothers and daughters in the street, at the park, in the supermarket. They were everywhere and over time these observations became too hard to bear, too raw to acknowledge, and so I cast my eyes downward and chose not to look anymore. In the same year that my brother was born, over 3,000 kilometres away my mother gave birth to another daughter. The gap left for me seemed to be growing smaller still, while the longing in my heart only deepened.

At the age of ten my whole world was turned upside down when I was told that my mother would be moving overseas with her new husband and daughter, and the initial trauma of abandonment suddenly deepened. She would return to the country for the Christmas holiday period and I longed for those six weeks over the summer to arrive, year after year. I could hardly contain my excitement as I flipped over the calendar each year to December, for the counting was no longer in months but reduced to days. She did not know how much I needed her, and she never asked. Perhaps she thought a stepmother was all I needed and that she was no longer required in my life, made redundant by another woman's presence. How could anyone know how a child longs for their mother if they had never been left without one themselves? No one ever really asked me, ever. So, the fractal pattern of my mother leaving carved its presence into my soul and became the groove that I moved in, day after day, year after year. It became the cornerstone of our relationship. Still, I longed for a connection that was not mine to have and for years I cried myself to sleep, praying each night that one day I would feel the motherly love I longed for. That prayer was answered in time, I just didn't realise how long I would need to wait.

At the age of fourteen, something snapped inside of me as a deep realisation set in, one where I recognised the hopeless situation I was in. I remember this age as being a pivotal point for me emotionally - the age when I realised that any dream of her returning, was nothing but a pointless exercise, and that the tears cried each night would never bring her back. It was time for me to 'grow up.' How does a four-year-old inside a fourteen-year-old body grow up? She shuts everything down, buries it so deep that not even she knows where to find it.

I hardened my heart to the pain, built four walls around it and wrapped it up so tight that it would not move. I became the queen of ceremony orchestrating the most artistic of burials – six feet under and shoved into every dark corner I could possibly find. The pain was safe there and hidden where no one could see. There are too many burials to name each and every one, but some of the most prominent answered to Abandonment, Longing, Rejection, Unworthiness, Trust, and Loneliness. All wrapped up tight nesting in my body and eventually growing as I did into the seams of adulthood. Yet underneath these layers were the corpses, the shadows of my childhood that were dying to come out.

From the outside everything looked in place, every wound carefully covered in layers of wrapping, woven with threads of denial and justification. From this vantage point there were few imperfections, just a perfectly packaged good girl. I dismissed my early childhood trauma as nothing to complain about, frequently telling myself, "Things are not so bad for you, be grateful for what you have, a roof over your head, food on the table." This self-talk fed my illusion that I was fine and kept me on the straight and narrow when the tracks were anything but. I convinced myself that I was just like any other kid growing up and the only thing that made me different was that I did not live with my mother like all my friends did. I remember my embarrassment when people asked what had happened to my mother, I simply replied, "Oh, I lost her when I was four." Often, they were so shocked that they would just say sorry and quickly change the subject. It was easier for me to play along with their assumptions that she had passed away, for what would they really think of me if they knew that I was abandoned, not wanted anymore? From my perspective, surely, they would think that something was wrong with me if I could not even be loved by my own mother. What I dreaded most was when someone asked me how she died, for it was easier to let people think that was the case. When I explained that she did not die, that she left me when I was four, I was met with the same look of shock and disbelief, except this time there was no "I'm so sorry," or "That must be hard for you." The truth was met by silence, no comment, or at most, a low, almost inaudible, "Oh."

As I grew older I convinced myself that everything was fine, even though my heart knew this was not true, regularly reminded of my loss as I watched my friends with their own mothers, saw the relationships they had, the bond that was obvious – the one so foreign to me but so longed for. It was at these times that I truly felt alone in the world, that something I desperately needed was missing and yet so far out of my reach. Through a child's eyes this was my lot in life, my only reality and I knew no other. I didn't understand that the source of my 'missing' feeling was embedded in my heart and could not be filled by any rational explanation. It was a mother's love I missed and craved and if I had known where to find it I would have hunted from dusk to dawn, yet I did not know where to begin on such an epic adventure of the heart. It was beyond my capabilities as a child, I had no map let alone the ability to read it if it were placed in my hands. So I did what I could to emotionally survive and that was to keep wrapping up my wounds in the hope that they would heal in time and be left behind. Year after year I applied new bandages, new over old with loose ends tucked in so that the wound remained intact. To let it open up and breathe would be too much to bear, for if it did it would surely weep forever more and all that was holding me together would fall apart at the seams.

I played this role for forty years perfecting every act and scene, but the costume eventually wears thin when it is worn for so long, with holes appearing and loose threads snagging on the unexpected. I could no longer read the script I thought was mine. As a child, I had always believed in the notion of destiny and that something bigger was waiting for me. I knew that I just had to hang in there and one day I would have the fairy tale ending I had read about in storybooks. I longed for it, I dreamt about it, and happy endings occupied my thoughts throughout my childhood. These thoughts disappeared as I grew older, as life as an adult and mother required my undivided attention. I forgot about my dreams for a fairy tale ending, but it had not forgotten my heartfelt wish as a child, made under the stars each night as I said my prayers and hopped into bed, praying for my mother to return. It snuck up on me when my back was turned, while my attention was focused on more pressing matters; matters of life and death and preparing to say goodbye to a friend.

In the years leading up to Vanessa's passing, the pressures of life mounted, and in hindsight, it was only a matter of time before something gave. As a mother of two children, aged fifteen and ten, I was juggling many balls in the air, and they were getting heavier by the day. I worked in a high-pressure job, managing a team of people and constantly under pressure to perform, meet benchmarks, and be an attentive mother, wife and friend all at once. I spent every spare moment possible by Vanessa's bedside once she entered palliative care and did all that I could for her while I had the time to do so. I was stretched to an edge I never knew existed. My health and lifestyle were relegated to the back seat and my priorities were askew. I was floundering but did not have the wisdom or distance from the situation to see it. I had endured challenging moments in my life and to me this was just another that I would ride through, cope with and move on from, as hard as this would be. Once done, I would bury it all as only I knew how and continue, for this was my pattern and conditioning.

It was during this time that my body started to show signs of the relentless pressure. I was in pain from spending too many hours at the computer, my neck and shoulders tight from burning the candle at both ends and my whole body was crying out to stop, slow down and reassess. I didn't of course, there was too much to do, too much on my mind, too much to fix. I had always been the 'fixer' of things, for even as a child I tried to hold it all together, to keep the peace, to find happiness in any way I could. During this time with Vanessa, my inner ten-year-old self moved in and was running the show. Fixing things made me feel better and made me feel worthy. It gave me a sense of purpose if there was something I could do to help, to create any impression of harmony.

Eventually I sought osteopathic treatment for the pain and after almost a year of therapy a thought came to me one day as I lay on the table. I felt as though the current treatment I was receiving was not quite enough - that there was something deeper to be reached and this was not the only way. The word 'massage' popped into my head and I typically cast it out again, thinking the osteopath I was working with knew what she was doing. Then a minute later as I lay there, she said to me "You know, I think massage might help you." I laughed and told her that thought had just crossed my mind.

This was not an unusual occurrence for me as I have always been one to intuitively know what is right for me and receive messages of this kind, for want of a better word. Call it a hunch or insight, these moments in life have never let me down and have always steered me in the right direction. I listen to them (normally) and when I don't they keep coming, subtle at first and then like a sledgehammer if I refuse to sit up and take notice. In fact, the very osteopathic clinic I went to held a special meaning for me. It was linked to a dream that I had when I was about two weeks off from giving birth to my first child at home, almost fifteen years earlier.

It was winter, and I was collecting wood for the fire. A large piece lay resting against the door of the woodshed and with my arms full I moved it sideways with my foot so that I could close the door behind me. As my whole body was preparing for birth, I underestimated the potential strain this could cause to the soft tissue in my body, and the inside of my right leg reacted instantly with intense pain. I soon discovered I could barely walk, let alone comfortably give birth to my child at home. I tried everything I knew to help myself naturally and following a discussion with my midwife, she recommended I see someone as soon as possible. I had no time to lose. I would find someone in the phone book the following morning. That was my plan.

That night I went to bed and had a dream, which was not unusual for me as I have always been a vivid dreamer, particularly during my pregnancies, however this dream is one that I will always remember.

Aboriginal Elders

I am sitting by a fire with three Aboriginal men. We are talking at first and in time they begin to play music with a didgeridoo and clapping sticks while another holds a spear in his hand. The fire is warm, and sparks fly up into a night sky filled with stars. I look into the eyes of the Aboriginal elders sitting before me and I know I am somewhere special, somewhere sacred. They too look directly into my eyes with absolute love and mutual respect.

I woke suddenly from this dream, in the early hours of the morning with my whole body tingling from head to toe. The detail of the dream was etched in my memory and I remember wondering at the time whether my daughter I was carrying and the elders in this dream were connected in some way.

The next morning the pain in my leg had not eased, so I started scouting the phone book for a practitioner who could help. As I was scanning several possibilities, one advertisement seemed to jump off the page as though it was visually glowing. I didn't hesitate and dialled the number. The clinic was not far from my home, so it was ideal as I did not have to travel too far in discomfort. I had not been to see an osteopath before, so I told the receptionist my problem and she managed to squeeze me in later that morning, reassuring me that they would do all they could to help. I was relieved and only hoped they could work some magic and get my body back on track and ready for birth.

When I gingerly shuffled in to the reception area later that morning I literally stopped in my tracks and my jaw could have hit the floor, for there on the wall behind the receptionist hung a most welcome sight - a painting of three Aboriginal men sitting around a campfire. One was holding a didgeridoo, another with clapping sticks in his hands and the third holding a spear. My initial shock and disbelief was interrupted by the voice of the receptionist as she took my details and asked me to take a seat in the waiting room. Every part of me knew I was in the right place and that everything would be all right. For me, it was a confirmation that I had made the right decision. It was here that I would get the healing I needed, but little did I know at the time how far into my future this healing would extend.

So, as I lay there in the same clinic some fifteen years later and talking about massage with my osteopath, I knew that I should follow up on her suggestion for massage as a form of treatment and that it would be good for me. Just how good for me, I could never have guessed! I had not seen a massage therapist for years and so I asked my osteopath for a recommendation. She gave me the name of a clinic just around the corner and I scheduled an appointment for the following week.

We were both right. Massage helped relieve some of the pain and I started to feel more confident that this would work. My shoulder and arm were feeling better, but I still had a long way to go. The massage therapist working on me was good and I saw her several times over the next few weeks. However, when I turned up for my fourth appointment I discovered she was unwell, and so I was booked in to see another therapist at the centre. At first, I was a little disappointed as I was making progress and beginning to feel more comfortable with each session, but I decided to go with the recommendation and keep the momentum going. This was the day I first met Jasmin.

When Jasmin started to work on my body I knew straight away that she was perfect! She seemed to read my body like a book, knew exactly where to focus and seemed to connect with me on a subtler level. I could not put my finger on it, but I walked out feeling amazing. I knew I was in good hands. I continued to see her over the next few months and although I was improving slowly, fate or destiny (call it what you will) had other ideas.

It was in one of these sessions that Jasmin asked me if I had heard of Bowen Therapy. I had heard of it in passing but knew little about it. She suggested it could help my condition, as she too had experienced similar pain and had reaped many benefits from this form of treatment. "It's not for everyone" she told me, but she thought it was worth mentioning. She recommended I see a friend of hers, and at that point I could see no harm in doing so. I would give it a try. She said she would write down her number for me following my massage. So, as I dressed and gathered my things and went to leave, words seemed to flow from my mouth without thought and with an urgency that took me by surprise, "That number, of your friend, can I have it?" I asked almost forcefully which was completely out of character for me. Normally I would have let this slide, waited for the next time I saw her or consider it if it were ever mentioned again. I was not normally this forthcoming. Yet something compelled me to ask for it and when I held the number in my hand, I felt a sense of relief wash over me and that something necessary had shifted into place. When I reached my car I immediately pulled out my phone to make the call. Again, this is something I would have normally delayed for a while, mulled over, got around to in time. I was busy. I didn't have a lot of spare time.

I dialled the number and within a few rings Katerina answered my call, but I had not the slightest inkling that my whole world was about to turn upside down and inside out. Looking back at this time in my life, I can see that the Universe was working in marvellous ways to ensure that I was exactly where I needed to be, and that Katerina and I were meant to meet at this very point in time, that we were each other's answer to deep soulful healing. For both of us, the time was now. If I had made different choices at that time in my life, then perhaps our paths may never have crossed. It seems that the Aboriginal elders in my dream knew, and the advertising image that glowed from the pages of the phone book knew, and I have no doubt that an aspect of myself, my soul, also knew that I was destined to live my fairy tale ending. I had of course, turned only the first page, of what would reveal itself to be a most remarkable story of friendship and unconditional love.

Illusouly

When I was in my early twenties, a clairvoyant had once told me that I have certain gifts which will unfold in time with maturity. It was during an intense time of emotional turmoil with my husband, that these gifts were realised, the first of these gifts unfolding as communication with the unseen, also known as channelling. My first experience of this occurred one night as I watched tennis on the television. As I sat quietly in my armchair, a strong and persistent thought came to me to quickly find a pad and pencil, and so I rushed to find what I needed. I sat down with these things in hand and continued to watch the tennis when suddenly my hand started to write; it was a name. I looked to see what I had written on the page in front of me and could make out the word, Illusouly.

Deep within I felt a melting pot of emotions and questions. I asked "Who is Illusouly? How can I be communicating with something or someone I cannot see?" My hand continued to write, and Illusouly explained to me that she is my spirit guide. I could both hear her and feel her, as I was writing down the answers to the mounting questions inside my head. She went on to explain that we had made a contract in a time between lives, where she would support me through this transition and my life's difficulties. I learned from Illusouly that I have six guides, ready to support and guide me in any way I asked, yet they largely worked together as one. To say I was surprised and overwhelmed by this moment is an understatement, yet this experience opened me up to another dimension of love and complete openness.

It was not long after this initial experience when I started to draw pictures alongside the words, for many messages came through to me in this form. A most memorable example is one night when I sat down with a pencil and paper and drew a beautiful picture of three peas in a pod. I didn't understand at first what this related to, but the message became clear; that each pea represents a child that I have given birth to, but this was not the case at that time for I only had two children. I had no intention of having a third child, but soon discovered a short time later that I was indeed pregnant again.

Illusouly demonstrated to me through words and drawings examples of healing energy fields, and on one occasion brought my attention to a rose that was dying in a vase on my dining table. She asked me to concentrate with the intent to create healing energy in my hands. When I felt this was accomplished, she asked me to cup the flower between my hands gently and just know in my heart that the rose was fully alive. I kept my hands in this position for a while, cupped around the rose, and when the time felt right, I gently released my hands. To my amazement the rose appeared fully revitalised, as though I had only just picked it fresh from the garden. Illusouly told me that this was a demonstration of the way I would be using energy to help people one day, and I was delighted with this prospect. Over the months that followed, she also introduced me to the concept of reincarnation and past lives, and through both drawings and meditations, I was able to uncover stories about my own existence as a soul evolving throughout time, and how all of these lives were linked with a similar thread, largely relating to mothering, children and fighting a constant internal battle to be consciously free.

One night as I sat quietly drawing, the image of a woman's face began to emerge. She had long wavy hair and large sad eyes which revealed her story, and an old story it was. On finishing what I can only describe as a portrait, I thought "Who is this person?" My question was intuitively answered in a waking dream.

Egyptian Girl

"I am Manet, a young girl around 14-15 years of age living in Egypt around 2700 BC. I work as a servant girl for a noble couple." I receive an image of walking through the markets where I notice a group of soldiers standing. Their presence in the market captures my attention for this is an unusual occurrence. I have never seen soldiers in the market before. I continue with my business buying flowers and goods for the household, when suddenly I detect a different energy around me. I see there is a soldier who is watching me closely and so I continue quickly on my way. Without further warning I am grabbed from behind by the soldier and he drags me into an alley or laneway where I am sexually assaulted. I am in complete shock from this event and do not understand or process what has just occurred. I return to the house and in several months' time realise I am pregnant and carrying a child. In time I give birth to a baby girl. I am terrified and terribly confused about what to do. How am I to look after her? Will I be thrown out of the house? If that happens how will we survive? The noble couple I work for notice I am carrying a child and as the wife is barren they offer to take my daughter as their own. Although I know this is the best *outcome for both of us, I feel nothing but the shame of being violated and the guilt of abandoning the baby I am carrying.*

In my current life, the challenge seemed to be intertwined with the same notion – of living a life with compromise. The hardest times were yet to unfold, and even though my life's karmic debt was so called "over," the struggle to create my own life on my own terms seemed like an impossible task. I sensed that life as I knew it would change dramatically if I were to live my life on my own terms, and that people would be challenged and hurt by my decisions if I had enough courage to follow them through. I carried immense fear at the thought of doing it alone, of putting myself out there, when all I knew about life was being "Greek" and that I did not have the education or skills that would provide me with the opportunities to nourish my soul. My immediate challenge was to find a way to fit in with the world and live a life that would sustain my heart, mind and soul, as well as providing a home, food and security for my children. I questioned "Am I capable?" All my life I had been dependent on my parents, and then my husband. Could I possibly do this on my own?

What saddened me most is that I had the gift of education whisked from under me, and with it my self-confidence. I remember so clearly the joy as a twelve-year-old, knowing I was going to high school and excited about learning and feeling a sense of growing. I couldn't wait to hit the books and study and read so that I could learn. When I started high school, we were all placed into a common level for the first two years to determine what levels we would be taught for each subject. I was put into a French class! I was ecstatic, as I always loved the idea of conversing in different languages, hoping that the future would open for me to travel the world. Despite these aspirations, I was not supported in any way by my family, especially one of my brothers who saw no sense in studying at all.

His attitude was most challenging throughout my teenage years when we were all working in the family fish and chip shop together. He was almost ten years older than me and insisted that I work in the shop from the minute I got off the school bus until we closed shop after 10pm. If I didn't obey his demands he would become very angry and aggressive, verbally abusive, and at times physically abuse me if I challenged him. He was relentless to the point where I had exhausted my energies on this level and couldn't fight anymore. There was no other way than to submit to his demands. I endured this for four years and would often turn to my mother and father for support, but they never responded in the way that I needed them to. As a result, I found myself struggling for time to study throughout my high school years.

I could have been an accomplished student for I loved all my subjects, especially maths and science, art, music and of course French and English. Even as I am writing these words, I feel my inner twelve-year old's sense of loss and deprivation at this point in life. Around me I could see girls were enjoying life in their teens, whether it be high achieving sportswomen, girlfriends socialising, going on holidays, talking about the boys they had met and the movies they had seen. I was envious, and I didn't dare mention my life or my family. I was ashamed that we just couldn't seem to 'get it together'. I felt deeply embarrassed and inferior as I compared my life as "Greek versus Aussie." It is no wonder I lacked the self-confidence at this critical junction in my life, and the ability to make life-changing decisions. I had never had the opportunity to practice good decision-making, let alone learn from them.

Unexpectedly, I now found myself in a situation where I was receiving guidance that I knew aligned with everything I was feeling on the inside. It resonated in a way that I had never felt before and gave me the courage I needed to step forward and take a leap of faith – into a future of my own making. However, despite Illusouly's beautiful presence in my life, I still needed to remain grounded and exist in the 'real world' of course. To explain to someone else the inner workings of my mind and spirit would only cause chaos and alarm, for I didn't fully understand myself what was unfolding. I knew that the guidance I was receiving was not coming from something external, but from a place deep within myself. This voice of calm and reason was accessible in a quiet space, where I was free to just be and have no other demands. To honour this space, I began a daily routine of walking in the early hours of the morning before my young family awoke. I would return home to a quiet household and meditate for half an hour or so, then with a pencil and paper in hand, I would be ready to write down any inspiration or guidance that would follow.

Through these experiences I learned to trust my own inner guidance, and in time there was no doubt in my mind what was right for me. I was being called by something much bigger, and I could not turn away from it, just as I could see that Kirsten was being called to tap into her intuitive wisdom and embark on some much-needed healing. As our sessions together continued, I was witnessing Kirsten's ability to connect more readily with her own inner wisdom and intuition. She was paying attention and linking her dreams and insights to her spiritual growth and her own ability to heal deep, deep wounds.

In fact, she reminded me of myself in so many ways and my own awakening to gifts I never knew I had.

Since she first told me her experience of her mother leaving when she was just four years old, a part of me so desperately wanted to share with her my own story; that I was a mother, who just like hers, chose to leave. The veil was beginning to lift, and I could see that the time was approaching when I would need to meet Kirsten eye to eye. I knew I had to do this sensitively, and time after time the guilt rose inside my throat, but I could not let it spill thoughtlessly. Kirsten had displayed her trust in me, otherwise I doubt she would ever have shared her story, and I felt like a complete fraud sitting in front of her hiding more than she could possibly realise. Here I faced a dilemma, one of telling her and taking the risk that she would never want to see me again but knowing in my heart that our meeting could provide us both with invaluable opportunities to heal our wounds.

I sat with this notion for some time, although I knew there was only a small window in which to act before her story unravelled any further. In the silence of my home I thought about what approach I could take. This was a delicate operation and one which required the utmost sensitivity and an open heart. The possible scenarios weighed on my mind, as did the guilt on my shoulders and the heaviness in my heart as the familiar and painful story rose to the surface again. I had so many thoughts running wild in this aloneness. Would she understand? Would she ask why I hadn't told her sooner? Would her anger rise like a storm and would she walk out of the room and leave me behind in disgust? Would she feel betrayed? I had so many questions, yet I knew there was only one answer, and that was to tell her my story, and the truth, that the person she trusted most to help her through this phase of her life, resembled that which she was trying so hard to make peace with. I couldn't let this go on for a moment longer.

Scraping it off Bones

"How do you always know what to say?
In that space of the black and the white,
where light and shadow dance on the edges of grey,
sharp and cutting
like some words can be.

But yours,
they are not like this.
They are as gentle as the spirit of mother,
soft, like mountain rain seeping through skin,
subtle, like the passing of time on any given day.

Yours,
Reach places unknown to most,
where a gentle breeze can move mountains
yet still hold a candle in the wind."

Kirsten Leggett

"I need to tell you something." Katerina told me, one day during a treatment. "Can we go out for lunch perhaps and talk?"
The first thought that entered my head was, "What is it that she has to tell me that we can't discuss here? What is it that she

knows that I do not?" My mind was reeling. It had to be significant – and it was.

In the months leading up to this we had talked about many things and I was beginning to see that we viewed the world in a very similar way. The significance of dreams, finely tuned intuition and spiritual experiences were all things we had in common with each other. She was open to these conversations and nothing surprised her, she never questioned the truth or the validity of my own experience, as many others had in the past. In fact, she seemed excited about them and communicated the same sense of wonder and intrigue as I did. There were few people in my life who I could talk very openly to about my dreams and who understood their significance and meaning. I had long shut this aspect of myself away from most, for fear of being judged or seen as weird, for this had been my experience since the age of fifteen when I started dreaming of events that would take place in the world, days or sometimes weeks later. I could dream of an earthquake, a tsunami, a mass shooting somewhere in the world. For some unknown reason I would dream of these events in the days leading up to them actually happening. At fifteen, I did not have the maturity to understand, nor did anyone I know have the ears to listen or provide me with an explanation as to why I was dreaming in this way. I see now that it was unfathomable to them, for it was outside their own experience. I soon learned to shut it down and ignore my dreams, put them down to coincidence, and eventually they subsided and became less frequent. I had switched on my self-doubt button.

Once married, I was fortunate to be able to talk with my husband about these things as he had witnessed first-hand the prophetic nature of my dreams, especially those with distinct warnings and dreams of conversations with family members who had passed away. Now, standing before me, was someone who was sharing her own stories of this nature and who listened so carefully to her finely tuned inner voice. She knew exactly where I was coming from and I felt free to share the unexplainable without having to justify or defend myself. I was free to be me, and I had much to learn from her. It did not take long before I felt like a student entering a classroom every time I walked through her door – and teacher she became.

In the following week we met as planned for lunch in a local café. I was nervous for I had no idea what was about to be shared, but I sensed it would be life changing. It was here she calmly told me her story. I remember every word perfectly. "I don't know how this will affect our relationship, but I need to tell you something." My mind was spinning as to what this could possibly be. I was preparing myself for rejection and thought that surely, she does not want to see me anymore, particularly after my recent emotional outburst about my mother. Perhaps I am more than she wants to be dealing with as part of her practice. I was already preparing myself mentally for this rejection. She continued, "I don't normally share this with many people." Instantly I was curious and then, as I sat there opposite her barely breathing, she started to tell me how that she too had left her three children when they were young. Two daughters and a son, and a carbon copy of my own experience with my sister and brother. As I sat motionless while I listened to her story, she told me her reasons, how hard it was and how her dreams and intuition played a big role in this. She told me how the messages she received were loud and strong and there came a point in her life where she could ignore them no longer. I wanted to hear more of her story and soon felt like a stunned rabbit in headlights as the significance of this information started to seep in.

The outcome of this conversation could have gone either way and we both knew it, but I felt nothing but respect for Katerina and for sharing this very personal experience of her life with me. She was under no obligation to do so, but I appreciated her honesty and this moment shared allowed me a glimpse into the other side; one from a mother's perspective, and the many reasons why a mother may choose to leave her children. I had long forgiven my mother for leaving me, but I had never had the opportunity to hear it from the other side, and so it was here in a quaint suburban café that a new door had opened for my understanding.

My own mother had never explained, never really sat down with me and talked about that time in her life. It may have been too hard for her to explain, the emotions still too raw, but the abandoned child within me needed to hear those words that were never spoken. It was only in this conversation with

Katerina that I began to see the trauma that a mother experiences in making the decision to leave and the deep conflict and guilt that is left in its wake. There is always a reason, and the decision to leave is never an easy one. On my drive home that day, the enormity of our connection hit home, and I was overcome with a deep knowing that we were meant to walk into each other's lives, right now, at this point in time. For me, there was no turning back or walking away – there was something more. I could feel it, like a ripple below the surface. Something extraordinary was unfolding and I wanted to be part of it.

From here on it felt like I had my foot planted on the accelerator and things were changing – fast. My life as I knew it was being cast to the four winds and I had no idea when or where I was going to land. The processing of grief was taking its toll on my wellbeing and I knew it was time to step down from my existing management role within the company that I worked for. The responsibility and pressure were too much for me to handle emotionally and I could not be there fully for those in my team. I was starting to implode. One morning I woke up and made the decision to commit to what felt right, to follow my instincts and inform my manager of my decision to step down from my current role and resume my former position in the company. I told no one else, not even those in my team. Then completely out of the blue, on that very morning I logged on to my computer to find an unexpected email from a former client gauging my interest in working for them. A new position had been created and they thought I would be perfect for it. It was one of those sledgehammer moments. Everything was pointing to the need for change and every cell in my body shouted YES! I jumped ship, released my sails into a different breeze and set my sights on a new shore. It was the course change I needed to find calmer waters – and my way home.

My sessions with Katerina continued to intensify and each time I saw her something within me seemed to shift a little more. As we talked, the crack inside widened allowing a little more light to shine in. I may as well have been lying there as flesh and bone as she seemed to see right into that crack and draw something else out, another memory, another piece of the sadness that was holding me together. She was the ultimate surgeon during these times, steadfast and reassuring; ready for just about anything that would surface. The memories did not let go of their hold on me easily and seemed to swirl around and around in my body looking for a way out. It was a whirlpool in there, and even when the words did rise to my throat, they would get stuck, imprisoned by fear. Fear that the child within would not be heard, fear that it was too late, fear of letting go to all that was me – for it was all that I knew. It was like scraping flesh off bones.

It was not only the childhood memories of being abandoned that brought me to my knees, but the deep longing of all that I had missed out on, especially the moments in my life when I needed my mother, and she wasn't there. I was grieving that loss too, the loss of what I would never have. Everywhere I went I noticed them, mothers and daughters sharing experiences together. I longed for the closeness, the connection. I longed to belong.

It was hard to sit with the gnarly bits and return to my four-year-old self. In the beginning I held back, largely in fear of where I might go, how deep it would be and how long I would remain there. It was one thing to be there in the moment with support and immediate guidance, but a completely different scenario when I walked out the door and needed to hold it together on my own. On some occasions it took me weeks to move through something and to find balance again. In the back of my mind I was also worried that the depth of hurt surfacing would feel like punishment for Katerina, for I could see now how my own story could resonate with that of her own children, even though their outcome was very different to mine. It could not have been easy for her to watch it from the other side. I did not want to hurt her in any way, so I held on a little more and told myself it was not important. The past is the past after all. Despite this, she encouraged me to dig that little bit deeper and touch it, feel into it some more in order to accept it and eventually let it go. She too, showed great courage in these moments.

Then in the midst of all the doubting that this was doing me any good at all, that it was all too much for both of us, my dreams started to tell me otherwise. Indeed, they were filled with messages that I was on the right track, and that we both needed to see and experience all that was unfolding; that the acknowledging and letting go was absolutely necessary for deep healing, on both sides.

Turn the Page

I am in a classroom and behind me stands a male teacher. In my hands I hold a large book which is heavy and fills my arms. It is my book, the story of my life, this life. I hold a page in my hand almost afraid to turn it over. I am hesitating and as my hand gently holds the page my teacher stands behind me whispering, "You need to turn the page. Katerina needs to see the next page also. You need to do this for her as much as for yourself."

On waking from this dream I knew that both of us had much to learn from the unravelling, that indeed I needed to go on and not shy away from my four year old feelings, and so I nervously accepted that it was time for a journey back in time, and that I would be dedicated to this journey and pay attention to every fork in the road; any signpost that would lead me to her place of hiding. It was during this time that I had a most significant dream, one that clearly showed me the direction I needed to go. That this emotional junction was so critical and that doors would open if I was brave enough to turn the knob and open them wide.

The Waiting Room

I am standing in a white space as though I am in the midst of clouds. I am waiting for something, anything or anyone who can tell me where I am. I feel lost. A figure appears before me and slowly the cloudy haze around him disappears. He is distinctly Asian in appearance and wears a robe. I recognise him as a Shinto Buddhist monk. We make eye contact, he nods as if to acknowledge my presence and gestures his hand forward signalling me to follow him. We walk slowly and mindfully forward until a path appears beneath my feet. Again, he turns to look at me and gestures his hand forward again. I can read in his eyes his message for me. "This is the path you need to be walking on right now." I continue to follow him until we reach the base of an enormous wooden staircase. Here we meet a woman dressed in vibrant blue. The monk fades away as the woman takes me by the hand and we begin to slowly climb the staircase. When we reach the landing I immediately turn towards the right. It seemed so natural, the way things have always been done. Yet I hear her thoughts in this dream, "No, not that way, we are going this way today," and she stretches her arm and hand out towards the left. I am surprised and a little intrigued, so I follow her direction.

We arrive at a long corridor. It is narrow and seems to extend such a long way, and at the very end of the corridor I see a small window with blue sky and sunlight shining through. The wooden floor is lined with an ancient rug and I step onto it cautiously. The small window gets closer and closer as I walk, and I am eager to look through it to see what is on the other side. As I get closer a large wooden door appears on my right. It is thick and solid and twice the size of a regular door. The woman in blue stands beside me and indicates there is something she *needs me to see. I stand silently and look up at the solid wood in front of me and notice there is a deep and intricate carving embedded in the grain. I can't help but run my hands over it. I close my eyes so that I can commit every detail of this fine and elaborate work to memory, my fingers reading it like braille. I sense a deep message within, that this place, this door I have come to holds great wisdom. There is much to learn by crossing this threshold.*

My hands find their way to a large door knob in the very centre of the door. It is so large that I need to hold it with both hands to open it. It takes much effort and the door is so heavy, but I put all my weight behind it and I push it open. On the other side of this door I find myself in a waiting room. It is comfortable, furnished with lounges and chairs that border a beautiful Persian rug featured in the centre of the room. I wait a while taking in the detail of this room, until the woman in blue tells me it is time to go in. She leads me to yet another door and as I follow her through I find myself in a room that is filled with the most beautiful and radiant white light. I sense another woman in the room, yet I cannot see her with my eyes, she is pure energy and holds great wisdom. I feel honoured to be in her presence. Everything is bathed in brightness and I can barely make out any features in the room, it is so bright, but I can hear her voice clearly. She welcomes me, and I sit quietly on the chair that stands behind me.

The moment is suddenly interrupted by a loud knock on the door beside me. I jump, a little startled and wonder who has followed me here. I am a little fearful and I ask out loud to the wise woman, "Who is that?" She pauses, and I hear her repeat those words to me, "Yes, who IS that? Why don't you open the door and see for yourself?" I am frozen to the spot and all I feel is fear. "Go on," she says reassuringly, "Just open it, you have nothing to lose." I get up from my seat and move towards the door. My hand reaches out for the handle, but I cannot bring myself to turn it. As my hand hovers there I notice there is a large gap under the door and so I drop to my hands and knees to peer under it, and my eyes widen when I see who is on the other side. It is my mother and a tiny four-year-old girl playing with toys on the carpet. I recognise the four-year-old as me.

I wake suddenly from this dream with the realisation of all that it was showing me. Intuitively I knew that it was time to delve more deeply into what my four-year-old self needed. She had been sitting in the waiting room all this time, and that I need not be fearful anymore. I needed to find the courage to open the door and let her in. She was part of my soul who was lost. She had been left behind at the age of four when her mother had left, so traumatised by her leaving that she remained in the only place she felt safe, at an age when her mother was still present in her life. The dream was showing me she needed to come back home. Robert Moss describes this concept beautifully in his book *Dreaming the Soul Back Home* where he states, "Beyond the first room that the dream door opens are larger spaces, where the healing and soul recovery you are seeking may be found."[iv] It was clear from this dream that my seeking was over. I had found my four-year-old and she was my starting point. Now all I had to do was to figure out how to safely bring her home.

From the moment I accepted this and the commitment it would require, I began to feel something change within me; a certain lightness that followed after acknowledging emotions that had been shoved deep for way too long. Forty years of stuffing myself to the brim with sad memories and unspoken truths. It was Katerina who taught me the importance in acknowledging all that had occurred in my life, all the sadness and the tears; that the words long buried needed to be heard and beared witness to, and that there was nothing wrong with this. It was my truth. As too was my mother's truth – to leave me behind.

I entered some dark places during this time, and while I felt selfish for doing so, it was Katerina who reminded me that old grief needs to be dealt with. At times, the pit was so deep I wondered whether I would ever clamber out and over the edge again. In these moments I would remember her voice, a wise word here and there in conversation or another way to look at the emotion and just observe. Her voice was my companion in these moments, and her words a lifeline in which to pull myself out. No matter how deep I went, the threads were always there, dangling within my reach. All I had to do was hold onto one and haul myself up and out, one hand over the other. I have lost count as to how many times I needed that lifeline, but each time I found myself there the line seemed to get shorter and shorter and I spent less and less time in despair. As each memory was touched, I started to open a little more and as a result I started to see 'me' and not the shadow of the four-year-old girl, huddled in the corner with her heart wrapped in chains. I was learning how to reach in and grasp that little girl by the hand in order to bring her to the present.

We worked hard together, month after month, year after year, and with all the inner work going on it was no surprise that my dreaming also accelerated to reach new heights. In fact, we talked a lot about dreams together, for they held deep meaning for me and showed me the way into and out of, some of the darkest corners. They became the blueprint to understanding all that I was working through. I had always thought everyone dreamt like me, but the more that came to me on 'night shift,' the more I realised my dreams and the messages within were anything but ordinary. In fact, my first dream of Katerina, and an insight into her importance in my life, came early on in our relationship.

Meditation- the Teacher

In this dream, Katerina and I have a scheduled meeting and I am running late. She is waiting patiently for me on the top of a steep hill, sitting cross legged. Beside her I see the most radiant energy in the shape of a human being, male-like yet with no distinguishing features, just a beautiful bronze light sitting next to her. She appears peaceful and wise. Reaching her is hard work physically as the hill goes on and on, but I arrive at her feet with many apologies, puffing and out of breath. I become the student in front of the teacher. She calmly says to me, "It's okay, everything is all right. You know, you should meditate, it will be good for you."

At this point Katerina and I had not discussed meditation in any of our conversations, and I didn't know that she had practised meditation for years. I had practised meditation before I had my children, just here and there, but it had slipped away from my lifestyle as the busyness of raising a family took hold. When I told her of this dream we talked about meditation and its many benefits. She seemed surprised that I would dream this about her; a little intrigued almost. So, I listened to my inner voice and her advice in my dream and I began to meditate once more. I slipped back into it like an old glove and with it a commitment to this practice, which in turn enabled me to open yet another door to an even deeper aspect of understanding myself.

  I woke without effort early each morning so that I could have an hour of stillness before the demands of family life kicked in. Meditation was the icing on the cake and its inclusion in my life provided me with another tool in discovering my triggers and the way I operated in the world. I had been chipping away at the edges, and now I was getting ready to bring down the walls.

  I was opening up in ways I had not experienced, and it felt good and very necessary. I could not stop and the more I searched the more I found. It was liberating on so many levels. I knew in this moment that my life as I once knew it was never going to be the same again. I could not go back to who I was for the path back was gone. I was on a new trajectory. I knew I was on the cusp of something profound when I woke from a dream early one morning.

Free Falling

I see myself perched on the edge of a cliff with my back facing unfathomable depths. I stand there, with my heels hovering over the edge and my arms outstretched in the morning sun. There is a beautiful glow surrounding me and my long, blonde hair floats on the breeze around my face and down the back of a red dress I am wearing. This is not the 'me' as I see myself in the mirror, yet it is ME. With my eyes closed, I hover there, teetering on the edge, seemingly at peace with all that I am. Around my neck hangs a gold chain with a bright red ruby attached which rests against the centre of my chest.

As I stand there I hear a distant sound, so soft at first but becomes louder and louder as the beating of wings became apparent. I open my eyes to see what is coming and see a hawk approaching from a distance, its silhouette becoming larger and clearer with each beat of its wings. In no time it is so close, just metres away and with its talons outstretched and feet forward, our eyes lock, for just a split second, as it makes a direct line for the ruby around my neck. Its talons grip it tight as I am knocked backwards, and as it rips the chain from around my neck I begin to lose my balance. I move my arms back and forth to right myself, not dissimilar from the wings of the raptor in front of me, but I had reached the point of no return, and I knew it. I was about to take the plunge of a lifetime. The chain had been broken and I was now free to fall – into myself.

Dreams like this seemed to 'arrive' in those moments when I needed them most, when I was deeply searching for a reason or an answer to some of the bigger questions in my life. All I had to do was ask and I received answers. My favourite part of the day soon became bedtime. I had been journaling my dreams for many months, and the more I wrote the detail down, the more I understood what my dreams were trying to tell me; or show me. I was open to this and I soon became aware that it was me all this time who knew what was best, and what aspect of myself I needed to explore next. I was remembering how important it was to do my own inner work but most importantly, I was remembering how to be me – my true self. More and more seemed to unfold until I began to see patterns and triggers in my emotional wellbeing that were clearly linked to my past. Once I recognised this, I began to dissect that part of me to understand it from an experiential level and only then could I let it go. I could not change the past. I could only accept it as it was. My mantra during this time was one based on many conversations and words spoken with Katerina. It is what it is.

As I worked with Katerina through these insights, I learned first-hand that the physical body can hold onto trauma in the most incredible ways; we bury past hurt deep within ourselves. Here it manifests and grows to become embedded in our psyche and become triggers that set us on the path of the familiar and our conditioned responses. There is no right or wrong in this, and by observing it in this way, I no longer felt I had to keep it buried or place a cloak of denial over its head, because that is what is socially acceptable – when you're an adult. I needed to revisit the trauma of being four and being suddenly motherless, and my dreams continually reminded me of how important this was – that being un-mothered was a huge part of my life.

Himalaya Calls

As I began to see more and more of Kirsten's inner four-year-old, I was also bearing witness to the incredible wisdom that children hold within, and their ability to recognise that questions need to be asked and answers given. In a safe environment, where space is held for them, they are free to raise questions that weigh on their minds. Children are naturally intuitive and often more aware of what is going on in their surroundings than adults give them credit for and are often astutely aware of what events are about to unfold. In fact, my eldest daughter had predicted my leaving the family home, well before I had ever considered this a possibility.

One morning as I was making breakfast, my daughter approached me and asked, "Mummy, are you leaving us?" I was taken aback and didn't quite understand her question, so I asked her what she meant by this. She replied, "I had a dream last night," then paused. "Go on," I urged. *"I saw you walking alone along a beach. You came to the rocks along the shore and then walked out to the rocks that pointed out to the sea. You stood there for a while, gazing out over the water. You looked so far away. All of a sudden, a huge whale leaped out of the water in front of you and swallowed you up and swam away. This shocked me, and I woke up, and then I thought...Is mummy leaving us?"*

I was quite shocked by the symbolism of her dream and felt the need to defend myself, but I was unsure why. I blurted out quickly, "Don't worry sweetheart, it is just a silly dream." Yet inside I could feel my soul stirring, as if in acknowledgement of an idea already conceived, but at the time I thought this was so far from reality. No matter how many times I pushed this thought away, something would always surface to remind me again and again that things needed to change, and when I chose to ignore those intuitive moments, my dreams would show me exactly what I needed to see.

The Warning

I am working in our supermarket on a bright sunny day and everything is going as usual. My husband had left to purchase some fresh produce to sell in the shop. Some time has passed since he left, and I am feeling anxious but didn't understand why. A customer arrives in that moment looking very upset. He approaches me and pauses for a moment in silence. "What's the matter?" I ask hesitantly. He replies, " There's been a terrible accident on the highway...your husband was involved...I'm sorry to tell you, he's been killed!"

I snapped out of that dream in shock and immediately reached over to see if my husband was next to me. I knew it was a dream, but on another level, it answered a burning question. I knew in my heart that if we didn't separate that one of us would die, not necessarily physically, but that if I chose to stay in this marriage, I would die on the inside.

In a meditation one morning, I enquired some more and asked for clarification on the meaning of this dream. The answer came quickly, "Your husband in this dream represents you, working in the shop and not living the life you've been wanting. This existence is killing you, not him, and the choice to stay will eventually kill your creative nature. Should you stay, you will both experience this death, as neither of you would be happy living in a loveless relationship." This clarification was profound and even though we hadn't been getting on so well, I would never wish that existence upon him or myself. The decision to leave consumed me daily. I became despondent, desperate and so unsure about my life. It was an incredibly difficult time.

The children were in the middle of our controversy and I was very sensitive to their delicate natures, but my husband would have horrendous childish outbursts in front of them. I asked time and time again for him to take our issues into another room, not to air them in front of the children, but he insisted that if he wasn't happy, then they should not be happy either. I couldn't see the sense in this, but I could see that our current situation wasn't working. A major point of annoyance for my husband was a dirty messy house, but achieving an expectation of a tidy home was not easy with three young children. We had a beautiful home, high up on a hill with stunning views of the beach and river. It was the perfect setting from the outside looking in, but inside it was anything but harmonious.

I had been working as a massage therapist for a few months, when my employer mentioned he was holding a self-development seminar on meditation, and other themes around spiritual connection. I was very excited to attend, and so I approached my husband and asked for his permission to go. He was not at all pleased and was more concerned about who would take care of the children for the day, who would do the housecleaning and cook the meals. I promised him that all would be taken care of if I could attend. I arranged for my mother to take care of the children and as the day of the seminar arrived, I worked solidly until 3am to clean the house and cook the meals so that I would be free of household obligations, so that he would have nothing to complain about. I was both physically and emotionally exhausted.

The following day, I dropped the children off at my mothers and attended the seminar with my sister. The whole experience was incredible as I sat in a hall packed with like-minded people. I was enthralled from the very start, as we explored topics about reincarnation, meditation and spirit guidance, all of which confirmed Illusouly's teachings for me. When it was over, my sister and I collected my children who were already bathed and fed by my mother and returned home. When we arrived, my husband seemed calm and content with how the day had unfolded. I warmed up the lamb stew I had prepared the night before and the three of us sat down to eat. He didn't ask a single question about the seminar, so I let it pass. While I was washing up our dinner plates he asked me if I would like him to light the fire in the lounge room before we watched a movie. I told him I was exhausted from the day and wouldn't hold out much longer, but my sister, in her eighth month of pregnancy, offered to stay and watch the movie with him. I was relieved and retreated upstairs to our bedroom, brushed my teeth and went straight to bed. I fell asleep before my head hit the pillow.

I was woken suddenly with the abrupt and urgent words, "The fire, the fire, wake up!" I was dazed and disoriented as I emerged from a deep sleep to my husband yelling "Fire!" I jumped out of bed and responded with "Where, where, where's the fire? Where are the children?" I looked around frantically, to get my bearings, to see him standing in the middle of our bedroom staring at me. I asked urgently, "What's wrong, what's happened? You've woken me up about a fire. Where is the fire?" He responded by saying, "There is no fire. I lit the fire downstairs for nothing. Your sister went to bed. She just left me there."
"You wake me up in this manner to tell me this?" I couldn't believe his audacity. He thought nothing of it and disappeared into the bathroom. I was so angry about his behaviour, I grabbed a blanket and my pillow and went downstairs to the fireplace and made myself a bed. I laid down to sleep and within minutes he came storming downstairs, pulled the blankets off me and demanded that I return to our room upstairs. I had no intention of sleeping next to him that night, for he was too angry, and I felt

uncomfortable in his presence. I was exhausted, my energy spent and all I could do in that moment was sit on the arm chair and burst into tears.

I yelled at him "That's enough, I've had enough. I do not want to be married anymore. This is not working. I will take the children and leave tomorrow." It was the final straw. With this last comment, he broke down and cried and pleaded with me not to take the children from him, for he could not live without them and could not be without me or the children. He begged and begged me not to leave, and for the first time in my life I felt as though I had some control over my situation. I had the strength to make the decisions I needed to. Here was my window.

I sat quietly in thought for a while, then told him that I needed some time out to think about our future together. For three days I did not speak a word to him but sought the quiet inner space I needed in order to *feel* into what I needed to do. I had three adorable children and I knew I had to put their needs first. After three intense days I arrived at a conclusion, and it was then that I announced to him my terms. "I will give this marriage a second chance, one more year and if at the end of this year, whether you've changed or not is irrelevant to me, it is how I feel that is more important. If I don't feel love in my heart for you, and if this marriage is not true to my soul, then I shall move on with the children and we shall part."

The following year my husband was perfect. He was the model husband who could do no wrong. I continued to work as a massage therapist and I was enjoying all that I was learning. A colleague of mine, Christina, had recently returned from a trip overseas and was preparing her next trip to trek in the Himalayas. She generously invited me to join her on her next journey, but I explained to her that this would be impossible as my husband would never allow me to go. She kindly offered to talk to him, and so I agreed wishing her all the luck in the world! She did talk to him, and surprisingly, he said yes, I could go with her to Nepal. You could have knocked me over with a feather.

As I sat on the plane ready for this new and long-awaited adventure with my friend, I stared out the window to my three children and could feel the phantom umbilical cord stretching. I inwardly questioned, "How far can I go without it breaking?" I was on a plane about to travel half way across the planet, all the way to the Himalayas. It was my dream come true, one I had been longing for all my life and every cell in my body was ringing with joy. My husband of twelve and a half years "allowed" me to travel with my best friend to Nepal, to a country that sits in the centre of my soul. I had no idea why, but I had felt this beautiful country calling me for some time, and now I was on my way with my friend by my side. She had spent years travelling and exploring remote corners of the earth, and she inspired me to travel and explore in a similar way. As the aircraft accelerated and left the runway, I looked out the window one more time in the direction of my children, standing at the terminal window watching me leave. Lift off – and reality hit. This was the first time that I would be away from them. It will be four weeks until I will be able to physically embrace their little bodies into my arms again. Tears streamed down my face as the cord stretched longer.

Trekking in the Himalayas in those days was like a rite of passage. I thought it would change me for the better and this was my expectation; to return with a fresh outlook on life and a new understanding as to where I belonged in it all. I was twenty-nine years old and I was throwing myself in the deep end, for it was the first time I had ever left the safety of the country on my own and without my family - a time when every personal decision to be made was up to me. It was an exhilarating feeling. My parents were not very supportive of my choice to go on this journey, my mother especially thought my friend was a bad influence, but I ignored her remark. This was my opportunity to demonstrate to everyone that I could think for myself, make my own decisions and stand on my own two feet.

Throughout the long flight, I reflected on the eve of my departure and the last discussion I had had with my husband. We talked about the promise I made myself almost a year before and that this opportunity to travel independently was going to give me the space I needed, to look at us and our future and to see if there was a chance we could make our marriage work. It was not that I didn't love him, and it was not that we were wanting for anything; we had everything we needed. This was a decision that I alone had to make, and I was not blaming anyone else for how I felt. It was all me. I was confused, lost and had felt unbearably oppressed.

As our flight approached Kathmandu, I glanced out my window to see the most magnificent view – the Himalayas. It was breathtakingly beautiful in its enormity, with crystal white snow topping the peaks that are the highest in the world. I could easily recognise Mount Everest as it was the only peak on the range without snow, due to the strong winds that blew it away before it had time to settle and take hold. Time stood still as I was deeply moved, feeling privileged to witness such a majestic sight.

My first impression of Kathmandu was horrifying! After we cleared customs at the airport, we hopped on the first available bus into the city and were dropped off two kilometres away from the Kathmandu guest house, where we would be lodging. I threw on my backpack and followed Christina as she made her way around other travellers who were getting their bearings from maps and tourist brochures. Kathmandu was a backpacker's haven! So many young people descended on this city from all corners of the world, and while they all looked weary from their journey, their eyes showed nothing but an enthusiasm for adventure.

I followed Christina through the crowds, and we emerged onto the main road, where I struggled to comprehend what I was seeing. Right in front of me on the path and sitting on a dirty old rug, was a small girl no older than two years of age, looking straight at me with her tiny hands outstretched. I thought to myself and then voiced to Christina, "What is this? Why is this baby alone on the street, and where is her mother?"

I was promptly answered with "This child is a beggar, keep moving and don't stop." However, as we continued, the scene replayed itself over and over as we wound through the streets. I was bewildered by these sights and overwhelmed to see so many people living this way. I had not been prepared for this onslaught on my senses, or the realisation of my naivety. Christina was striding ahead of me with a clear intention to move as quickly as she could through this scene, one she was clearly familiar with. An English backpacker walking beside me tried to strike up a conversation, but I didn't hear a word of what he was saying. All I could hear was my heart pounding as I struggled to make sense of it all. Ignoring him, I kept moving and eventually caught up to Christina. She looked at me, as though she knew exactly what I was thinking, but didn't say another word. As we arrived at the guest house, I was relieved to find it was a little oasis tucked away from the suffering I had just witnessed, and as soon as we reached our room, I sat on the bed and cried. I wanted to go home.

    The Kathmandu guest House was an old palace in the Thamel region. It was rustic but quaint, and provided cheap backpacker's accommodation, with warm and friendly staff that couldn't do enough for us. We rented a cosy room with two single beds and settled down for the night. I was simply exhausted after the long and emotional flight, and went into a deep sleep very quickly, accompanied by an alarming dream.

Not Ready!

We are having a party at the Kathmandu guest house. There is a refrigerator and in the freezer compartment is some ice cream. I really feel like having some but a notice on the door prohibits anyone to eat it. I think about the ice cream and decided I would have some anyway. As I open the freezer a man appears, who is not very friendly, and growls at me to get away from the door. I ask why we aren't allowed to eat the ice cream, but he just pushes me away and yells "You're not ready yet!"

I woke face down on the bed and had an awful sensation that someone or something had grabbed me by the feet and was trying to pull me out of my body! I was frozen in fear and couldn't yell out for help, when suddenly in the darkness Christina jumped out of her bed and started to push the menacing energy away from me. I was physically shaking, and once fully awake and the event over, I praised Christina for her instinct, somehow, she knew I needed help even during deep sleep. We sat together for a while discussing my dream, when she turned and asked me what I was carrying with me emotionally. I remembered the words within my dream still ringing in my head, "*You're not ready yet.*" I just broke down and cried, and gradually opened up to her to tell her I was here to decide on the future of my marriage. She was astonished by this declaration, for despite her awareness of my marriage problems she hadn't thought it had come to this. She immediately jumped to a point of judgement and exclaimed, "How could you possibly even think of leaving your marriage, disrupting not only your lives but the children's, think of the children!" Consumed by a wave of guilt, I cried out to her in response "I'm not good enough!" As I sobbed she tried to console me by telling me that I was a wonderful mother, and that I really needed to take the time to think about my situation. However, I had no idea where to start or how to begin to deal with my core issue that had developed over many years - my lack of self-worth.

The same dream reoccurred a few times during our journey and presented itself when I was anxious about the decision I had to make, when I was struggling with my subconscious issues around self-worth. These issues had been part of my existence for as long as I could remember, and to step away from this belief was harder than I had ever anticipated.

The following day I was sitting in the court yard of the guest house surrounded by a lush green lawn, bordered with bright gold and orange marigolds. I sat at a small outdoor setting with a selection of postcards to write and send to my children. I loved nothing more than to connect with them in this way and as often as I could. I was happily writing and deep in thought when I was interrupted by a man named Paul. He was English, very friendly and open and looked typically 'hippy.' I felt comfortable with him, so when he asked if he could join me I obliged, and we sat and talked for a while. He shared stories about his life, his travels and the various experiences he had in different countries. He was passionate about conservation and living a natural life style, with the intent to minimise his footprint while exploring the world. I found him intriguing and the topic on conservation was inspiring. After a lengthy conversation, he extended an invitation for me to join him at a dinner party that evening and to bring my friend along too.

Later that night we met Paul at the restaurant as planned, where he introduced us to a table full of people from across the globe, travellers who were English, French, German and Dutch. Meeting people from such a range of nationalities was a new experience for me. Whenever I went out at home I was always with my husband, and then it was only with Greek people. Finding myself in a foreign country sitting at a table with total strangers from around the world was exhilarating, and I loved the atmosphere I found myself in. It felt natural to be here swapping stories and learning about other cultures, almost familiar in a sense. Then the realisation set in, that this had always been my childhood dream, to travel the world and experience the very thing I was immersed in right in this moment. I was happy; deeply happy, and wished that I could do this forever.

In this multicultural setting, I found myself sitting opposite an English man by the name of Chris, who was very articulate and seemed to know a lot about the mountains in Nepal. He and his friend Mathias were planning to undertake a 300 km trek across the Annapurna mountain range, over Thorang La, the highest point on the trail, and then descend to Muktinath. Christina and I were setting off in the opposite direction for Sagarmatha National Park, to trek to Kala Patthar (meaning Black Rock), a small mountain that provides a vantage point in which to view the peak of Mt Everest. This was the only location along our route in which to see this iconic peak, pending on the weather and how well we could acclimatise to the high altitude at 18,000 feet above sea level.

Chris was a hive of information. He'd been a traveller as a photojournalist for twelve years when I met him, and he simply loved what he did. The Himalaya was his favourite place by far, and he intrigued me with his stories and knowledge of a place that I also felt drawn to. I liked him, and our meeting triggered my recollection of a dream I had several months earlier as I prepared for this trip, about a journey and meeting a photographer, who I travelled the world with as his assistant. We connected immediately and had such a lovely time at the dinner party, where the topic of conversation was not about shop keepers, business or politics or the best way to make money, or where the women talked superficially about fashion and jewellery and the holidays they'd been on. It was so refreshing to discuss global issues, topics on conservation, culture, and of course the mountains. The Himalayas. My head was spinning. It was as though for the first time in my life I felt like I belonged, here with these genuine people who brought out the genuine me. I felt real.

The evening progressed quickly, and in no time at all it was time for us to leave. We needed a good night's rest to catch the 5am bus to Jiri, which comprised day one of our 26-day journey, and a nine-hour bus ride from Kathmandu. We said our goodbyes to the group, and by the time I reached Chris he asked me if he and Mathias could walk us back to the guest house, as they were staying there too. We talked some more as we made our way back under the brightness of a full moon. The streets were quiet but scattered with people who had made their beds on the hard ground, mat after mat stretching down the sides of buildings and spilling out onto the streets. I was instantly reminded that I was in the world's second poorest country, and deep within my heart I wanted to rescue them all. I discussed this with Chris, and he went on to explain to me that these people came from remote villages to make money during the tourist season. They did this by begging on the streets and would then return to their homes during the winter when it became too cold to sleep outside. He advised me not to give to those who begged, but to observe who the locals gave to, because they were the people who genuinely needed support.

My thoughts raced back to earlier that morning when Christina and I were walking through the streets, and were confronted with a sight we would never see on the streets at home, or ever forget. Before us on a mat lay a man with long dreadlocks wearing nothing but a pair of short pants. He was incredibly thin, and as he laid on his back he held a little drum in his right hand that looked like a rattle with two strings, and little balls attached to either side of the drum. With his other arm missing and both his legs amputated at the knees, he projected nothing but a sense of misery. Tears rolled down my face, as he held the handle of the drum and twisted it backward and forward beating, beating, beating tirelessly, trying to grasp the attention of all who passed him. I recalled the local Nepalese giving him money and food. He appeared to be well established on that corner of the footpath. As I dropped some rupees into his bowl my eyes met his; deep dark whirlpools of innocence and despair. I grew up in poverty, or so I had thought, but compared to this sight, I quickly realised that my insight into poverty had only just begun.

As we continued to walk back to the guest house that evening, I told Chris about this man we had seen on the street. Chris knew of him and acknowledged that he was the only person he gave money to. He warned me not to give to the small beggar children as they were strategically placed on their street mats every day by their parents, to collect money from the passing tourists who gave very generously. Unfortunately, this was causing many families to keep their children out of school, only to send them to the streets daily. My thoughts went directly to my children who were worlds apart from this existence, tucked up into their beds at night with a full tummy and a roof over their heads. The cultural shock of life in this country was sinking in, and I was beginning to feel home sick.

I learned quickly that the help these people needed most was from their own government, and that foreign assistance only ever offered a band aid solution. Many westerners have tried to help by building schools and orphanages, and providing water for remote villages, only to discover that the only way to gain support from the bureaucratic system, was to line their palms with bribes. Many organisations who have tried to help ran out of money before they could finish their projects, while some watched their dreams shatter, as newly constructed buildings were turned into tea houses or accommodation for trekkers, with all proceeds filling the pockets of bureaucrats! My head was spinning at how ignorant I had been about the plight of countries like this. My real education was only just beginning, and I had much to think about throughout the nine-hour bus trip the following day.

Our trek was physically challenging, and the first three days were the most difficult as our bodies adjusted to the demands of each day, however the scenery was entrancing and distracted us from the pain our bodies endured. At the end of each day Christina and I gave each other leg massages, the soreness and stiffness reminding us of the gruelling day to day challenge of trekking in this mountain range. Thank goodness I was travelling with a masseur! It was extremely challenging and pushed every edge of my resilience as I felt thrown in the deep end of this adventure, but I was happy, and frequently thought "If only my mother could see me now!"

One day during the trek, I became awash with a distinct feeling of Déjà vu. This wasn't unusual for me, but on this day, it was particularly intense as though I was walking into a distant memory. It was not long before the images and information started to roll in, from a past life as a Buddhist monk in Nepal. Christina and I had been travelling in the Khumbu region a few days, where we came across a Buddhist monastery in Tengboche. Christina was so enthused by the sight of the monastery and temple exclaiming how beautiful it was, but I did not share the same feeling. She beckoned me to come inside, but I had no interest whatsoever in following her. I suddenly felt uneasy and queasy in my gut, and my instinct was to leave this place quickly. She went ahead regardless, and so I had no other option than to wait patiently. I found a bit of earth to sit on amongst the rock and sat down as my head was spinning, I felt sick, and the uneasiness of this place felt all too familiar. I calmly closed my eyes, took a few deep breaths to relax my mind, and let the story unfold. As though I was watching an old movie, I began to understand the reasons for this sudden onset of anxiety.

Betrayal

I am living as a Buddhist Monk in the 12th Century and there is a problem with the teachings. A sect named the Mahayana have come to preach to us, hoping we will change our beliefs to mirror theirs. We are of the mind that our teachings are of the original Buddhist teachings of the Sakyamuni School of Thought, and to change any of it will be sacrilegious. I appear to be the Lama, or spiritual leader for our monastery and try very hard to convince the other monks to remain faithful to our pure teachings. Unfortunately, the majority are lured by the Mahayana philosophies and those of us who remain are suddenly at risk of losing our hold on the traditional teachings. I make a stand for those of us who remain loyal, and while I am confident I have made an impact, I am soon assassinated by poisoning.

No wonder I didn't want to go inside this place! The sense of betrayal and treachery from my own people of that time was still lingering. My body remembered, and so the feelings of fear, nausea and dizziness returned. Realising I needed to make peace with this place, I continued to sit and entered a deep meditation. Here I acknowledged the event for what it was, and the significance of the emotions I still carried since the day I was poisoned, and that life ended. I forgave those who were responsible, blessing them and the event, along with this place of memory. What followed was a deep sense of peace and as my heart opened, the fear, queasiness, and dizziness disappeared altogether. I felt lighter, relieved and a little overwhelmed by the whole experience. It also confirmed the strong pull I had felt for many years towards this country, and my unfinished business here, now resolved. It became clear to me why I feared speaking out for myself in this current life time, as the consequences of doing so bled through from my life as a Monk in the 12th Century. After this experience and the resulting insights, I was happy to explore the monastery and temples with Christina, all of it feeling incredibly familiar as I stepped back inside one more time.

The days trekking in the mountains provided space in which to lay out my thoughts, and the quiet moments in which to weigh up my choices. With each step forward, I became more certain about the path I needed to take. The path I was treading became a metaphor for the way I envisaged my future – I never knew what was coming around the next bend, what peak would present itself against the skyline, but I needed to keep taking a step forward, no matter how tough the journey became. It was these moments of clarity that shaped my fate, however I kept these thoughts to myself, for I needed to be sure. I had no idea how my decision making would unfold, or what it would look like. The last thing I wanted was to hurt anyone, but who was I kidding? That part was inevitable.

It was here, in the stillness of the Himalayas, that I could finally hear my voice clearly, and I knew that I could not return to be the person I was or the life I had been living. I just didn't fit in that world anymore. I missed my children so much while I was away, but unfortunately, I had not missed my husband at all. I was relieved to have some personal space and freedom and felt empowered on a level I had never experienced before. I felt safe to be me and make decisions on my own. I did not want to lose this feeling, now that I had it at my fingertips, and it was only a matter of time before I realised these feelings were confirming I needed to leave my marriage. Shockwaves of fear rolled through me, fear of the unknown and the turmoil that was about to unfold. How do I tell him? How will he respond? How will it affect the children? Of course, I had no answers to any of these questions.

Looking into this space was harder than I had ever imagined, and the fear of separation was overwhelming. I had never lived on my own before and had always had others make decisions for me. My children were so young, how would they cope with a separation? The sudden realisation of this responsibility and the consequences of my actions shook the foundations I had built my life on and had me trembling in my shoes. As I observed the four-year-old innocence in Kirsten and the emotional trauma that her mother leaving had caused, I was instantly drawn back to this moment in my life when agonising decisions were made. As Kirsten found the stillness in which to unravel and understand, I was hurtled headfirst into the fray of memories and the consequences of my heart wrenching decisions. We were both calm and storm, juxtaposed in our stories, yet united in this journey.

Surrender

*"The long fingers of the old crone
forge a ravine from my crown to toe.*

*An opening,
a chasm,
where emotion dwells,
memories filed.*

*Her whispered chant,
soft in my ear
weaves magic within.*

*Setting free and releasing
the trappings of humanness."*

Kirsten Leggett *(2016)*

It is in the quietness of our inner world where true healing can occur. When we cease the busyness and honour ourselves in a way so that we can feel into what is pulling us in for a closer look. Honouring this space is critical to reach the bottom of it all. To dip our toes in is not enough, we must allow the time and space in which to sink a little deeper, to submerge ourselves in the emotion and memories that are calling us. If we answer, and meet them half way, we can be blessed with the greatest gifts, those that lead us to experiencing a feeling of wholeness. I discovered this one day in my own half way house; in a place of realisation and profound beauty. I affectionately call it, my Orange Space.

I first encountered this beautiful space while attending a breath retreat. The Orange Space was not something I ever imagined existed, yet this extraordinary space I found myself in allowed me to shed yet another layer that had shielded the child within. One could liken it to peeling an orange, as I dug my nails in and pulled back the flesh to expose the white pithy bits underneath. Pungent and a little bit sour, it was the layer I needed to take a closer look at. I had never been to a breath retreat before and I was unprepared for where it would take me, but take me it did into the most necessary spaces. I entered this four-day retreat as a forty-five-year-old woman but emerged as a four-year-old girl. It may seem like a regression of sorts, but it was anything but, as it allowed me to truly return in a physical sense to a time in my life that I needed to feel again and experience, but within the safety net of a well-structured and supportive environment. Katerina attended the retreat with me, and knowing she was there added that extra layer of warmth and security. Her presence gave me the reassurance I needed to dive in to the depths I was only just beginning to discover.

Breath work is nothing short of miraculous in terms of its ability to heal and let the body process and move through all that it has held onto. I would never have imagined that the gentle act of breathing could bring about such transformational change and create a natural conduit for the release of so much more. In fact, my introduction to breath work was through Katerina, who in the early stages of our work together used this form of therapy to help me connect more deeply with that wounded part of myself. Even then, without fully understanding its power, it helped me to bypass all that was spinning in my mind and feel into what my body was holding onto.

Then, many months later and through a series of dreams, I felt guided to find and attend a women's circle. I was most surprised to find there was one in my area and it was here I first met Cindy, the facilitator of the circle and by chance, an experienced breath work practitioner. It was one winter Sunday during the circle that I noticed a beautiful poster on her wall promoting a breath work retreat scheduled for mid-spring. I brushed it aside thinking "Not yet, perhaps I need some more time," but it was already my time, I just didn't realise it. Coincidentally, a few weeks later, Katerina mentioned she would like to attend the retreat and asked me if I would consider coming too. It was all the encouragement I needed, and to know that she would be there gave me the courage to say YES!

I entered the retreat with eleven other people for a period of four days, tucked away in a beautiful location surrounded by nature and removed from the demands of caring for family and running a household. Here I had the time and space to just be, show up for myself and allow space for the unfolding. I had no idea that I would find the "Orange Space" here, deep in the heart of the forest where crystal cold waters lapped the river shoreline just metres from where the twelve of us held this space for each other. Most us were strangers, yet we were all there for the same purpose, to uncover that which we may not understand, or that which was too hard to face alone.

For my first breath session I sat with an older woman who I shared a room with. She was gentle and calm, and I sat next to her as she volunteered to breathe first. It all began as I expected, with music playing while six of us watched over our partners and the gentle rise and fall of their chests. I sat quietly next to my breathing partner watching and waiting for anything, but all seemed perfectly calm – for now.

The sudden noise from behind me took me by complete surprise as one of the participants began to wail. The pain in her heart was palpable and my whole body stiffened as I felt the wave of anguish wash over me from behind. My body shivered as goose bumps enveloped me and deep within, my stomach clenched, and my heart rate quickened. I had not expected the impact of this moment and the intensity of the energy that filled the room, and as I looked around me, many others were entering this zone I had never encountered before. Thoughts raced through my head, "Is this is where it will take me? Can I really let go to this level?" and no sooner had these thoughts come and gone, when I heard Katerina vocalise her own emotions in that moment from the other side of the room. I felt conflicted and fearful of where this might take me. Did I cause her to feel such pain? Am I responsible in some way? We had shared so much, but was my story affecting Katerina in ways I could not possibly know? Guilt began to surface.

When it was my turn to breathe, I entered the space quietly. I was a little apprehensive and there was much noise going on around me by this stage as people connected with deep and raw emotion, but despite this I felt calm and centred. As my session progressed I could feel myself becoming lighter and lighter as a fresh energy rippled throughout my body as though it was trying to find a way out through my skin, a tiny space in which it could be set free. I had a river of memories and emotion washing over me, but the current was on the surface only. It felt so real I could have reached out and touched it, but I had not yet reached the depths of where I needed to go. I didn't have the skills or the confidence to take the plunge, not in that moment. This session passed with ease and a gentleness which left me feeling a little perplexed, but calm and grounded also. I wondered why I wasn't feeling the depth and intensity of the breath that so many seemed to be exploring around me. Would this be my experience for the following three days? Perhaps I wasn't as ready as I thought.

Katerina asked me if I would partner with her in our next breath session the following morning, and although I was still a little nervous at what might unfold, I felt safe – to dive a little deeper this time knowing Katerina would be right there. I had no expectations and perhaps this session would be no different from the last, but I remained open to the experience and was excited to be sharing this moment with her. We had done this before, so I knew everything would be okay, and I lay down on my mattress and began to breathe. Everything seemed quicker this time around, as though the pathway had already been worn and I could feel the ripples of the undercurrent that were once on the surface, pulling me deeper. Then part of me would panic, and I would resurface, block it all out once more, only to be pulled under again. I felt like I was being tumbled about in a whirlpool, trying to make sense of this place and I had no idea which way was up. After a while I reached a tipping point, a point of no control, where my mind completely stepped out of the way and my body took over, as though it too had a mind of its own. This terrain wasn't unfamiliar as I had been here before in sessions with Katerina, but it was different this time, more intense as though fuelled by some unseen gravitational pull. I was entering a new space; that much I could feel, and I was subconsciously feeling for my life line, that invisible cord I could pull myself back up on if I needed, but this time it was not within my grasp.

    All I can remember is that it was dark, I was confused, and an inner battle was underway between wanting to leave and wanting to stay. I was in fight or flight mode and I was frightened, I felt so small, like a young child searching for comfort after waking from a bad dream. I felt as though I was running down the longest and darkest corridor. Instinctively my whole body turned over and I desperately wanted to bury myself deep within the mattress I laid on, I was blindly searching for a burrow, a place in the earth that would swallow me whole. As panic set in, I became aware of the most beautiful energy beside me and like the gravitational pull of an undercurrent, I was pulled towards the right. The sensation was magnetic as my whole body moved of its own accord in that direction. In this moment it felt as though I had no control over my movements and my body was searching for what it needed most. This place was drawing me in and like a baby, I raised myself on all fours and put one hand in front of the other and crawled towards this beautiful tranquil space that I could sense was within my reach. I did not stop until I found the source of this beautiful energy, Katerina, and tucked myself into her lap, small and tiny like the young girl I had returned to in this moment. There I was held, soothed and nurtured in mother arms while I cried. I surrendered to this moment, to the one I had so desperately needed when I was four – the one my whole body and soul ached for.

There, in Katerina's arms, I slipped into a space which seemed to have no beginning and no end, and I was floating, just being, like an unborn child in her mother's womb, and womb-like it was as I became encased in the most beautiful orange light which was filled to the brim with love. After forty-five years of being lost, I felt I had finally returned home – to the Orange Space. A space that perhaps we have long forgotten ever existed, but it is one we all started out from, a place of belonging and great love.

I didn't want to leave, and I would have stayed there in that space for the rest of the retreat if that had been possible. I had reached a place so deep, a place of deep wounding, that I had long shut out of my life for it was too much to bear. The intense longing for a mother's love coursed through my veins, it was in every cell of my body and was a longing I had denied, dismissed and thought I could move through life without. I couldn't have been more wrong. Katerina had shown me exactly what my body was searching for – she provided the safe environment I needed to acknowledge my loss and touch the pain my four-year-old self had not been able to hold. It was the most beautiful moment of realisation and no other person in the world could have done this for me. It was only she who had the deep longing herself, to understand this loss, through the eyes and heart of a child.

It was not until many years later that I realised the significance of this event in my life, while I was reading Edward Tick's *Practice of Dream Healing*[v]. He describes that there is "the period of nurturing and bonding, lingering in the sanctuary grounds in order to improve the details of living, seek relief in a safe place, and strengthen and prepare both psyche and body for more difficult healing work." When I read these words, I could see so clearly how Katerina had provided me with the emotional sanctuary I needed to move deeper, she was the place I would find both relief and strength to go on. Tick also states that, "finally there is a call to descend into the unconscious and return to the womb where the original wound is festering, awaiting a healing visit, and to heal our intractable wounds, we must return to the womb of our wound." There was no doubt in my mind that my Orange Space was exactly that.

From that moment on I wanted to touch every corner and feel every aspect of this union between mother and child. I needed to understand all that I had lost, all that was fragmented so that I could begin to put it back together again. I didn't want to forget a single moment, and so I began to write, and it was through words that I gradually began to understand a part of myself, the four-year-old and her needs, and that she had a right and an inherent need to grieve for all that she had lost, all that she had missed as she grew into her adult body. Through words and dreams my inner child called, and because I was listening, she was choosing to step closer.

Somehow, words would form from a place beyond thought, and unfold to provide me with the answers I was looking for. For me, words were, and still are, the keys that can unlock the heaviest of doors. I have always known that I write so that I may understand. The importance of writing for my own healing became evident one night when I woke in the early hours of the morning to find myself writing down words on the notepad beside my bed before quickly returning to a deep sleep. In the morning when I woke, I had a vague memory of writing something down during the night, a word or two perhaps. In fact, there were many and I was completely surprised by what I found there. Words, strung together so eloquently and with an inner wisdom that didn't seem mine. It was mine of course, and I had tapped into an inner wisdom and creativity I never knew I had. The more I wrote, the more I dreamt, and the more I dreamt the more I continued to write. There seemed to be a constant flow of words inside me, coming out in the most beautiful way. Words developed into hundreds of poems and in turn captured the songs from my heart. They became my medicine and key to understanding all that I was working through.

I was opening up now even as I slept. This opening, so evident by one of the most powerful dreams I can recall and will never forget– a visit from the old crone; the wise woman within. Clarissa Pinkola Estes refers to her as *La Loba*[vi] in her book *Women Who Run with the* Wolves, and is the old woman who lives in a hidden place within yet is rarely seen. She sings over bones using her soul-voice where on the breath, the truth of one's power and one's need is made known, so that it can be restored. I had the pleasure of meeting *La Loba* one night, in the midst of a dream and it was here that she showed me exactly what I needed to do.

The Contract

I am going to see Katerina for a treatment, although as it is so often in dreams, her house as I know it is completely different, located in a forest setting with floor to ceiling windows and large tree trunks in the middle of the entrance room. I glance out through the windows into the depths of the most beautiful forest. She asks me to sign in to the session we are about to have and passes me a notepad with three distinct columns. I can see where I need to write my name and I follow the line across the page to the third column where my signature is required. I notice in this column the word Mutar has already been written. I acknowledge the word and scribble my signature down beside it.

Once I sign the form, Katerina invites me to walk up a few wooden stairs into her treatment room and I follow her instruction. The room is darker than the entrance, but candlelit and there are ancient rugs with intricate patterns covering the wooden floor. On a low wooden ledge, I notice a number of ceramic green lotus plants with a beautiful light radiating from within each centre. I pick one up and hold it in both hands. It is warm to the touch. "Oh, they're beautiful," I comment to Katerina over my shoulder. She agrees and then suggests that I get myself ready and on the table; that she will be back in a moment. As I return the lotus light to its ledge I notice another 'me' almost sister like appear out of nowhere and she sits on the lounge that is in the room. Her features started to change, and her face swivels from the front of her head to the back, repeatedly like a hologram. I begin to panic at this point and scream out to her over and over "What are you doing here, why are you here?" She does not answer but only continues to change from what appears to be a young child to a woman. At this point in the dream I become frightened and call out for Katerina, over and over.

Katerina quickly appears back in the room and tells me it is okay, that everything will be alright and invites me to settle on the table. I do so with her gentle guidance and reassurance. Then, as I lay there on my back something extraordinary happens. I close my eyes and feel a sense of something very powerful wash over me, followed by a soft song-like chanting. I open my eyes, just slightly to see Katerina change and transform into an old crone, a medicine woman. Her long fingers are outstretched over my body and her face close to mine, her long grey hair brushes across my skin. Her face, hovers just above mine so that I can feel her breath on the surface of my skin. As she chants words I do not understand, she places her index finger on the crown of my head and then slowly draws a line down the centre of my body from head to navel. In this moment I feel my body completely open as though I have been cut in two equal halves to lay open on the table before her. The most intense feeling erupts from deep within and I weep and weep like a baby, as though every emotion I have ever held onto is released in that moment. When I stop crying, I open my eyes slowly to see that the old crone has disappeared and has transformed back into Katerina and the body and face I know. She looks at me and smiles with absolute love.

I woke suddenly from this dream with my skin tingling from head to toe and immediately wrote down every detail. It was hours before I could verbalise this dream as I tried to get my head around what I had just experienced on night shift. I knew I had dreamt something extraordinary and I replayed it over and over in my head so that I would not lose the detail. I wondered if *Mutar* was even a word and so with great curiosity I jumped online. I looked up the meaning and was astounded to read it meant *mutate* in Spanish. In this dream, on a subconscious level I had signed a contract to change; not just on the surface but at the very core of who I was, and I could read Spanish! I knew at this point that my relationship with Katerina was critical to this process. In hindsight, I had made a contract with her to help me find the missing part of myself. She was the one that would open me up wide enough so that I would have the ability to look deep inside; and the table, like the one in her room, was not so dissimilar from an operating table for the child within. I had committed to healing myself from the inside out.

Many years later the profound nature of this dream continued to surface and remind me of the inherent wisdom that lies within. This dream held many messages for me at the time even though I was just beginning to explore what lay beneath the surface. In fact, four years on I came across an article on the relationship with Self which triggered the strong memories of this dream. The article began with a story about a young monk who was sent into the city from his mountain temple by his master. The monk found it difficult to meditate amidst the noise of the city and became very agitated and distracted. He found meditation almost impossible so returned to his master in the mountains and told him of his struggles. His master listened intently and then, poking him in the chest, replied "What are you doing out there, when you should be in here?" His master was referring to the "light within the lotus," the same light within the lotus lamps I saw in my dream in Katerina's waiting room and held warmly in my hands. The "light within the lotus" is an old

Hindu wisdom teaching and refers to the place where our ego-self (the I, me, mine) merges with the transcendent self that we can lose sight of because we are so busy going outside, instead of staying to see what lies within. There was no doubt from this dream that I was being told in no uncertain terms to go deeper within, to keep stripping back the layers until I reached the very core, the epicentre of who I am. I was embarking on a rich journey that much I knew, for my dreams kept telling me to keep moving, keep travelling towards the next destination.

It's the Journey...not the Destination

I am waiting for the train that feels like it will never come. I take in my surrounds, an elderly man stands to my left in a worn coat, a garment loved over the years no doubt, as it has sheltered him from the elements of nature. I see a thread unravelled here and there. It is missing a button, but it looks like a second skin on him, as though it is part of him, tales of his life interwoven within the fabric itself. A small child on my right bounces a ball in her hand, the rhythmic sound of it hitting the platform is reminiscent of the passing of time, like the ticking of a clock. The girl looks up at the arrival board willing the train to come. I sense her eagerness to continue the journey and I wonder who will be on the other end to greet her. Will it be her mother's arms and her wide smile, or perhaps a friend, waiting excitedly in anticipation of what adventures the day will bring?

I sense the train approaching and I know that it is almost time. There is no looking back for this journey will take me to unknown places and I am ready to leave behind all that I know. It is not easy this change, for it is human nature to hold on to what we know. It is the comfortable space we grow accustomed to, a place bound by the walls of predictability. I feel the vibration of the train approaching through my feet, planted firmly on the platform beneath me. We all look up, expectantly, to catch the first glimpse of our ride. It is the light I see first, just around the bend in the tunnel as though it is showing me the way, drawing me in to the realm of possibilities. The hot air from the tunnel pushes forward, propelled by the momentum of what is to come, and I feel it arrive like a hot wind on my face. I close my eyes momentarily to prepare myself. My stomach feels tight and I reach out to touch a nearby bench to steady myself. I hear the train stop, just as I expect it to and I open my eyes in time to see the doors slide open, an invitation to my next stop, "Destination unknown."

I could write a book alone on my dreams and have had so many that are worthy of retelling. Sometimes they are short and sharp (the sledgehammer moments), and at other times they are long drawn out stories which ultimately lead me to what I need to see or know. As my dreams increased in their richness and clarity I decided to write my own dream declaration which I repeated each night before sleep, always ending with the words "Show me what I need to see." My dreams always delivered, every single time. I have a distinct feeling that washes over me after a dream that I MUST pay attention to. These types of dreams are the most profound, the timeliest and the most needed. Times when I need reminding that I am loved, I am capable, and that I have all the tools I need within my reach.

Torchlight

I am visiting Katerina and her partner where they live in a beautiful cottage deep in the forest. My visit has come to an end and it is time for me to leave and find my way home. I say my goodbyes and I stumble out of the front door into darkness and the smell of a cool temperate forest. Night has fallen, and I cannot see very well. It is so dark that I stumble and fall over tree roots along the track. I get down on my hands and knees and feel my way for the track through the forest floor. I am a little frightened by the absolute darkness I find myself in. I suddenly remember that there is a light in my pocket and I just need to locate it and remember how to turn it on. I try to open my eyes to see a little clearer so that I can locate the light, but they are heavy with sadness and grief. Even though I know the light is there, I do not have the strength at this time to open my eyes and see. I eventually wake within this dream to find myself nestled in the highest part of a tree, a large and old Eucalypt. There is softness at my feet, like fur, which rouses me from a deep sleep. I open my eyes and it is morning and I feel a certain sense of relief that I am safe and nurtured in the arms of this tree and Mother Earth herself.

I look across from me to another huge Eucalypt that stands opposite me, and there nestling in its branches is an old but wise Koala. She talks to me as she chews on Eucalypt leaves and tells me that it is truly amazing that I have reached where I am with no light, even though it was in my pocket all this time. She then glances out over the horizon and over the highest branches to the most beautiful sunrise I have ever seen. A majestic landscape reveals itself under the subtle morning light. The Koala proceeds to tell me to rest a while and now that daylight has arrived I will see where I am going and trust that the earth will take care of me. She looks back at me and as her Koala eyes meet mine I felt so protected, nurtured and safe. I remember the light in my pocket and know I can reach in and grab it whenever I need. That I am to rely on it during the darkest times, so that I can find my way home.

I woke from this dream knowing that all I needed was within my grasp. The light I needed to draw on was within me. I paid attention to every dream I recalled and listened to the messages within, for the more I listened, the deeper I seemed to delve, and in time my dreaming took me places that I would never have thought possible – into lives I have lived across time. How did I know these were past lives? Every part of me knew as though I was flicking through the pages of an old photograph album. I could read and understand languages foreign to me and recognised key features of landscapes I had never visited. It was as though certain events in my current life and the stripping back of emotional layers were triggering memories from lifetimes ago. It was in such a dream that I first reconnected with a past life, at the time of my death. It was short, sharp and hit me with such force that I felt shaken to the core.

Lost

I am hovering an inch or two over her face; her blue eyes open to the night sky and a thin line of blood seeping from the corner of her mouth. She is me, and I her, a waif-like teenage girl lying alone on the cobblestones, drenched in winter rain. There is something about the separation from this body that feels premature – she has run out of time. Her thin body is clearly malnourished and dressed in her only belongings, the clothes she wears, worn and grey and not dissimilar to the night sky she lay under. She dies alone; no arms to hold her or wipe the damp hair from her face. She was searching – that much I know, for the ache in my chest tells me so, as does the sadness in her eyes.

I woke from this dream and sat bolt upright with my body tingling from head to toe and gasping for breath. This was my first conscious recall of a past life in a dream. I can't explain how I knew she was me or the story that led her there, but I liken it to pulling out an old movie and pressing play after years of being stored in the back of a cupboard. I had a vague memory of the setting, the character and the hardships she had endured. I was living in Ireland or England sometime in the 1700s – over 200 years ago. I did not know my name at this point (this comes in a later dream), but I knew my feelings to be true. I had been separated from a life and someone I was not yet ready to leave behind.

I talked to Katerina about this during my next session with her and she suggested that this dream may indicate something unresolved, perhaps some unfinished business in a past life. At this point I had no idea what that was or whether I would ever find out, or even dream of this girl again. The furthest thing from my mind was that Katerina was part of this story also.

Separation

Over time, and through the sharing of dreams and memories, I began to realise that abrupt separation was a deep and painful memory for Kirsten on so many levels and resulted in a fear of abandonment. She began to share more and more, and as we explored this together, I was continually reminded of my own heart wrenching decision to separate myself from my children. I felt that the reason these events in Kirsten's life had such a profound and long-lasting impact was because she had never been told why this had happened or received verbal reassurance that she was loved. I could see that her four-year-old was struggling to find peace with it all. At the same time, I witnessed the progress she was making, and it was astounding. I couldn't help but wonder how her life may have been different if she had heard these words as a child.

For me, I understood that each of my three children would have their own interpretation as to why I returned from the Himalayas, only to leave them with their father, and that they would each draw their own conclusions from this event over time. I also knew the moment would arise when they needed to hear my version of the story, to help them understand the reasons why I left them. Up until this point they had only ever heard their father's version of the story. This moment came five years after I'd returned from the Himalayas, and had left my marriage and the home that my children continued to share with their father. At this time, I was fully aware that on a subconscious level they would still be feeling the trauma of separation five years on, and that I, being the one who caused this trauma, would ironically be the one who would need to answer questions, with the hope of assisting them in their healing.

That time came for me one lovely spring day, as my children and I were on our way to visit their grandparents. My eldest daughter, now fifteen, always had plenty to talk about, but on this day she seemed particularly quiet. I could sense that something was not quite right, as her energy and mood was intense. I asked her if there was anything on her mind, and she flatly said "No". I asked her if she had a problem she needed help with at school, and she replied that there was no problem. I found her resistance to respond to me disconcerting.

Finally, we arrived at my parents' home and knowing how astutely intuitive and sensitive my mother was to other people's feelings, I was reluctant to take them straight into the house. Arousing my mother's attention on this issue was the last thing I needed, for I would never hear the end of it. So, I asked the children to just sit with me in the car for a few minutes before we went inside. I sensed what was going on, my daughter's emotions were palpable, and the best thing I could do for her was to give her permission to let out her anger. If I let this moment pass now, her feelings would remain invalidated, and this rift could continue well into her future. Fifteen can be a very precarious age, and the last thing I wanted was to see her coping with her emotional pain in this way, by holding it in and potentially leading her down a path of self-destruction. I looked at her and softly said, "Come on sweetheart, I know you're holding onto your feelings. You can express them, especially if they concern me."

She looked over at me with an intense glare, but I was unprepared for what came next. She let out a primordial scream unlike any scream I had ever heard before and it made the hair on the back of my neck stand on end. It seemed to go on for a very long time, but in reality it was less than half a minute, eventually subsiding into a gentle sob. Her big brown eyes brimming with tears looked at me as she yelled, "Is this what you want from me? Are you happy now?" and without interruption she continued, "All this time you've been away from home, do you think it was easy for me? I've had to look after my brother and sister, and it's been so hard being their Mum! I've had to work in Dad's shop after school and on holidays! I haven't been able to play school sports on the weekends! It's been so hard for me and I've been so angry at you!" There it lay, so very clearly, as I witnessed her raw anger and grief caused by me leaving, and it ripped through my heart. She sobbed a little while longer, which gave me time to gather my senses while she calmed down. There were no other words to say other than, "I'm so, so sorry! My intentions were never meant to cause you or the younger ones any harm or grief! I knew it would be difficult, but not like this." Once more, I felt the weight of unbearable guilt and shame. She had every right to be angry at me and I apologised again and tried to explain to her that I never intended to leave them with their father. I didn't want to blame anyone, but they needed to hear the truth and the reasons why I left. I realised now how important it was for her, to understand this story once and for all – to see it from both sides.

I explained that every decision I had made was with the intention to leave the children as unscathed as possible. I didn't want to be one of those parents who exploit their children, like pawns in a game of chess and drag them through the courts, creating more insecurity just for the benefit of financial gain. I did my best not to degrade her father as I explained to her how he refused, under any circumstances, to leave the family home so I could stay with them. He had threatened to make things difficult for me by selling everything we'd worked for over the years, including the house, and would not assist me financially in any way to provide a safe and secure home for us. I didn't want to take them from the only home they knew, or from their schools and friends. It was hard enough that a separation was occurring, let alone strip away the life as they knew it.

He had threatened to drag me through the court system and make life as miserable as possible for us if I resisted. I could not do that to them. I felt a well of emotions rising and tried very hard to suppress the flow of tears. I had never dreamt it would be this hard for my eldest daughter. With sincerity, I explained that making the decision to leave them behind was the most difficult decision I had ever made in my life, and that when the time came to tell their father he could have custody, I just couldn't find the words, that I had stuttered and coughed, and still I couldn't let the words be spoken. Eventually, I broke down under pressure, until the words I dreaded most tumbled out of my mouth. I felt sick to my core that day, and everything about the situation felt deeply wrong. Something within me died.

I told her how devastated and confused I was, not wanting to ruin my children's lives but their father's as well, because this decision was not his choice, and I felt a responsibility to make sure everyone would remain as unscathed as possible. I continued to tell her that I hadn't anticipated the aftermath of my decision. My family was so disappointed in me, and my mother wouldn't talk to me for months afterwards. I was ostracised by the Greek community, who blamed my friend Christina, as they believed it was her who led me astray. She was spat on in the street, and blamed and shamed as the culprit, as though I could not possibly have made this decision on my own. This treatment of her was demoralising and unforgivable, as the decision was mine alone and was not influenced by her in any way. I shared with my daughter how alone I had felt without my children, and the tears I shed day and night for years on end. All I wanted was to be with them, and that seeing them on weekends was never enough. Even though the suffering was killing me inside I could not go back to live with their father.

With that as my reality, I felt that the best option was to leave the country for a while and allow the volcano that had just erupted in my life to settle down. I felt the Himalayas calling me once again so I returned to the country where I had first found my freedom, for solace and healing time, and while I had travelled back and forth regularly to see them over the years, I understood that it was no compensation for my constant presence in their lives. Now that I had returned home for good, I expected to pick up from where I left off, but it wasn't so easy. Hearing my daughter's side of the story was heart wrenching, and parallel to my own teenage years, working days on end in a shop and not experiencing life as a teenager should. What could I do or say to make amends? How could I have let this happen to her? Another layer of guilt, shame and lack of self-worth was created that day.

I was astonished that my daughter, along with the little ones, sat and listened to all I had to say without a word, and once I had finished talking, she looked at me and said calmly "It's ok mum." I reached out to them all, and we held each other in a long loving embrace. I could only hope that this conversation was of immense value to them, and that they would never think they were to blame in any way. I could see that this was just the beginning, but at least it was a step in the right direction. From that time on, I would remember to regularly check in on all three of my children, to ensure their feelings were heard, and allow them the time and the freedom to express themselves, and to validate their self-worth with reassuring love.

I have often reflected on how I got to be where I am today, observing as far back as I can remember to the present moment in time. I have asked myself, "How did I ever get into this mess? Why do I react the way I do to situations that annoy me or I feel threatened by?" I have come to know, through my clients and personally, that every trauma we've ever experienced has been recorded in our body's cellular structure. From the moment of conception, to floating around in the safety of the womb, to being born into an environment filled with noise and bright lights. The body remembers the impact of this transition, our first inhalation and shock of breathing, and our instinct guiding us to search for the source we've been torn from. Every cell in our body remembers the moment of the first embrace into the warmth and security of our mother's arms. Birth itself can be experienced as trauma for a new born baby, and this trauma may be as simple as being separated from the security and safety of its mother's womb. A newborn child may experience for the first time feelings of abandonment, helplessness, aloneness and fear. A mother's bonding love at this time is paramount to a child's well-being and is the lifeline on which he or she depends for survival.

My level of understanding deepened unexpectedly during a weekend training course called 'Mind Body Bowen,' a non-invasive body therapy which I include in my practice. It is a deeply healing therapy, which facilitates the body's ability to tap into its cellular memory, to connect to issues that may be impacting overall health and well-being. I entered this session with another course attendee, with no expectation or preconceived ideas on what issues might arise for me during the process. I was most surprised by the experience and the state of awareness I found myself in within minutes, recalling not only my body's memory of physical birth, but my experience within the womb, and outside the womb prior to conception! I experienced these intense sensations physically within my body, not as a meditation or a dream, but as a cellular memory of the birth, and separation from a place of warmth and love. For me, it was most distressing as I felt the depth of the emotional trauma at being separated from my mother, and it was here, in a locale of the soul, that I could begin to understand how separation at any age, could inflict deep and lasting wounds. It has shed light and understanding as to the depths of suffering a child may endure when a mother suddenly becomes absent in their lives, and how this trauma can continue to live on in the body, until the long-suffering child can be retrieved. Retrieval may come in many forms, and there are many different modalities in which to approach this, but ultimately it takes great courage, enduring compassion and faith that a child will always find its way home, where they will be received with love.

I knew in my heart that Kirsten had the courage to find her lost and abandoned four-year-old and I was prepared to do anything to help her. We had come this far, and I sensed that I too, would find healing in this journey, and it was one I felt compelled to be part of. The connection I felt with Kirsten was now so far beyond the client-therapist relationship. I could feel a bigger story unravelling for both of us. At the time, I was lost for words as to what this might be, all I knew was that I felt I owed it to her; to guide, reassure and welcome her home.

Just for the Record

*"We have journeyed before you and I
Travellers with no destination,
a ticket to the unknown.*

*You have shown me the way,
then and now,
gently guiding with compassion and love.*

*I sense this, even though I cannot be sure,
for my soul knows this story,
like a memory discovered in a dream."*

Kirsten Leggett *(2016)*

As my sessions continued with Katerina, I felt more at home in her presence, and as our connection grew stronger the more we opened and shared. I couldn't explain why I felt so connected to Katerina, but I felt such a sense of belonging when I was with her. I did know that our meeting was meant to be, and that she would be the one to help me heal, find my lost child within and help me bring her home. Still, I had many questions that remained unanswered about my feelings and dreams about her, and felt at a loss as to where to begin.

One morning, I happened to be connecting with a friend on Facebook when I read a statement she had posted about another friend's work. "This is the greatest gift you can give yourself," she wrote. I was intrigued, so I read on. I was struggling to nurture my own inner child at the time and I was searching for anything that would make a difference; to help shift the old grief that had its grip on me. I had been advised that is what I needed to do; to reach in and bring the small child within me home, but I didn't know how to do this or where to start and I was struggling. The gift my friend was referring to, was a reading on your own Akashic Records. I had heard of the Records, many years ago, but had never dived into this aspect of knowing myself. I was unsure and quickly dismissed the thought. Then day after day the words kept popping into my head, and life's little synchronicities kept nudging me in this direction, so I followed my instincts and investigated it some more. I was a good researcher, a trait perfected throughout years at university and I left no stone unturned.

Akasha is a Sanskrit derived word meaning "space" or "sky" and can be described as a compendium of your own thoughts, words and actions that are stored and encoded on the astral plane as energetic events and described as the universe's super computer system; the central store house of all information for every individual who has ever lived on earth[vii]. They are records that are relevant to your soul's journey since its inception, recording all its knowledge and experiences from the past, present and future[viii]. The Records can be accessed through a meditative state to learn more about yourself, your purpose and life experiences and to gain insight into that which is most helpful. It is yet another way to understand the significance of why you may be at a particular junction in life.

As soon as I read the word Sanskrit I had goose bumps all over my body, for I had experienced many dreams where I was reading Sanskrit, often words carved in stone and glowing in a golden light. I understood the language while dreaming, although the meaning dissolved quickly when I awoke. Similarly, I had experienced many dreams where I am scanning through library shelves looking for 'records' and have observed books glowing on the shelves; ones I must take and add to the pile in my arms to aid my understanding. I had never fully understood the meaning of these dreams, but believe they were steering me in the direction for that very moment; when the opportunity to look within on another level presented itself. I took this as a sign I was on the right track. I wanted to know more about my own Records and it felt so right at this time. I booked in a session to occur over Skype and would see what unfolded. I was nervous, but I had nothing to lose.

My first reading with Michelle absolutely blew me away. I talked of my grief, my losses in this life and the questions I had in all that I was working through with my own feelings of abandonment and deep longing for mothering. I had never met Michelle prior to the reading, we had never spoken or conversed in any way, yet she knew traits about me that she could not have possibly known. There were so many moments within and after the session that Michelle calls "Aha" moments. Moments where the penny drops, so to speak, and everything falls into place; integrates. In the days and weeks that followed my reading, the inner turmoil settled, and I experienced moments of great clarity into why I was feeling the way I did, why certain things rattled me so. I felt lightness like no other and my heart, finally not so heavy. I liken it to being shown the most beautiful path, signposted to the way home after a long absence. We touched on past lives during the reading and her account of these too made perfect sense. It was like finding that piece of the puzzle that had been cast to the corner of the room and now retrieved, coated in layers of dust. My reading was like blowing that dust covering clean and seeing the picture underneath for the first time. I could now see a part of the puzzle unfolding – the picture was forming. It was the picture of me.

During this reading, Michelle was repeating, almost verbatim, words and complete sentences that Katerina had spoken to me during some of our treatment sessions. I said to her surprisingly "Yes, I have been told that," a number of times, and "Yes, I have heard that too!" After the third or fourth time she questioned who I had heard these words from. When I told her about Katerina, she asked me, "Would you like to know more about her?" I was hesitant at first, but the word *yes* was out of my mouth before I could give it a second thought. She proceeded to tell me an account of a past life that we had shared together as teacher and student, healer and assistant, surrogate mother and child. In that lifetime Katerina and I were part of the same clan where she was a medicine woman/healer/midwife who had assisted me many times during childbirth. As a way of thanks and gratitude I repaid her with my time and support in preparing medicine, collecting herbs and learning about healing. She was my teacher then, and surrogate mother as my own mother had died when I was young. In fact, that has been my pattern for many lifetimes; to be motherless. I knew this past lifetime connection was correct, not only as I was head to toe in goose bumps, but it triggered the memory of a dream I had several months before.

Inside the Adobe

I am sitting in a tub of water inside a hut with both earthen walls and floor. I can see animal skins and herbs in bottles and a low light filtering through from a gap above in this dome shaped hut. As I sit in the half-filled tub of water, my long dark hair falls around my shoulders and in front of my face as my head bends forward. My hair is wet I can see, as I look out to take in my surrounds through the long, dark strands. What I recognise most is the feeling in this dream; a contemplative quietness and inward reflection. Then, behind me I hear a familiar voice. It is Katerina's, softly spoken and reassuring as she gently washes my back.

I had just received my first piece of the puzzle about why I felt so connected to Katerina on so many levels.

As I continued to share my dreams with Katerina and my writing during night shift, the more words and images seemed to come. My writing became prolific and in time the words would not only surface during sleep, but in waking moments too and in no time at all I could almost feel their imminent arrival. A notepad and pencil were never far from my reach so that I was always ready, for the words would come quickly and would be gone again in a moment. It was like fishing on the side of a fast-flowing river; the words floating past, and me with my net ready for the catching. If I did not stop what I was doing to catch the words, they were swept away with the current and difficult to retrieve. I still have these experiences today, although with less frequency, but the intensity remains. These days I can almost feel their imminent arrival as though something is brewing. Then, when the moment is right, all it takes is a few words to filter in and then the flow is unstoppable.

Memories from past lives would occasionally surface in dreams when I was working through something particularly challenging on an emotional level, or when I inwardly enquired about why I was feeling a certain way about something or someone. They would shed light on an issue I could not work through easily or logically in my waking life, as though the relevance of a situation provided the catalyst for recall. Joan Grant alluded to this herself in her autobiography "Far Memory" where she states, "relevance, I've just realised, is a decisive factor, the tuning-mechanism."[ix] At other times, recall of events were more subtle; a flash of a landscape scene, an image of me washing my hands in a stream, picking up seed pods that had washed ashore, or running my hands over an artefact completely foreign to me in this life. Robert Moss refers to these experiences as constant "bleed-throughs", rarely noticed by humans on the ground, except in dreams that are frequently forgotten."

I once experienced a "bleed-through" of this nature while awake in my late twenties as I was collecting sticks for the fire along a country road outside my home. It was winter and late afternoon and I held a small bundle of kindling in my arms. As I bent down to collect another stick from the ground I saw dirty feet where my shoes once were and a ragged looking grey skirt instead of the jeans I was wearing. Grasping the bundle in both arms I noticed my once clean fingernails were now dirty and worn, attached to hands that did not appear to be mine. This image lasted all but a few seconds, but it stopped me in my tracks and I stood there motionless on the side of the road as my brain tried to comprehend what had just happened. I thought then, past life? Then put it down to the inexplicable and continued on my way.

The more I talked to Katerina over the months that followed about these events, the more she seemed to appear in my dreams. She would often speak quietly to me or I would be talking to her on the phone, and just as it was in my waking life, her words were always reassuring and her presence always powerful. We began to connect too in other ways that were outside of dreaming. I would be thinking of her and then in seconds receive a text message, and vice versa. We would both sense when something was amiss with each other and she always knew when I was struggling with something on a deep emotional level. We visited each other in dreams and at times I could retell events that had recently occurred in her life without actually being there, as this information came to me down the dream line. Distance seemed irrelevant for even if I was on the other side of the world in another country, I could still tune in to all that she was feeling on an emotional level. Our personal lines of communication were well and truly open and there was definitely no static on this line! It was clear to both of us that we were connecting with each other in extraordinary ways.

Despite this, as my appointments with Katerina continued, something unsettling seemed to stir and rise to the surface after each visit. At first, I could not make sense of the feeling, but it was intense; strange and familiar all at the same time. I had worked through so much already and I could not easily identify what it could possibly be, surely, I had touched it all. What else could there be? My first encounter of this feeling came several days after an appointment. At the time, it was difficult to name and put my finger on, but it soon became evident that it stemmed from a deep sense of longing; a 'missing' feeling that was encased in fear. The need to 'hold on' was phenomenal and my dreams were filled with the words, "Please don't go, please don't leave me." I brushed it away in the typical ceremonial fashion. Why would I be feeling like this about Katerina? None of it made sense, so I threw it in with the rest of my non-mothered baggage. Then week after week and month after month this feeling persisted and intensified even more until it surfaced the next day after treatment, then the night of the treatment, then at the bottom of the street just following treatment, and in time, just as I walked out her door and closed it behind me. I never uttered a word of this to Katerina for it felt childish and just plain weird, but clearly my instincts were telling me to stop and take a closer look. I had no answer for it and I had never felt this way before, about anyone. The longing to be near her again was so profound it was debilitating and took me days, sometimes weeks to recover from. I was in foreign territory and I didn't understand how I got there.

It was at this point I knew I needed guidance, and with the profound insight that came with my first Akashic Record reading, I was ready to explore this issue some more. I wanted to understand so that I could find the tools in which to manage these intense feelings, particularly the fear of loss as it was paralysing, but most of all, it was the burning question of why was I feeling this way? So, I dived in with Michelle again as my guide and it soon became clear. Every word that was spoken resonated so strongly within and the feelings were named. I cried and cried as the story unfolded and my heart remembered, in fact my soul remembered.

We talked of a past life where I was living as a young child in an Irish orphanage, and Katerina was there also, working as a nun. She had arrived, after she lost her own son in infancy. She was grieving and went to work at the orphanage to distract her from the pain of loss and to give what she could to children in need. She and I connected instantly in this life and she loved me from the moment she laid eyes on me. However, it was forbidden for the nuns to show any affection to the orphans, and so any moment of closeness was behind closed doors and shrouded in secrecy. For ten years, she loved me as her own and I helped ease the pain of her own loss, as she too filled the space in my heart where a mother's love would have been. As I approached sixteen years of age, she left without warning and without a goodbye for reasons unknown to me. I did not live for much longer after her leaving and died from illness and a broken heart. The "Aha" moment surfaced along with the realisation of an old and profound love. The urgency and panic I felt every time I left Katerina's room was that memory of uncertainty and loss resurfacing. I did not want to be left behind again. It was more than I could possibly bear.

    I sat with this a while, months in fact, and never spoke a word of it to Katerina. My own reading is just that; my own reading and I did not want to influence the development of any relationship with something that is tied to a single, barely tangible experience. So, I tried to integrate it as best I could, and the intensity in those moments of leaving Katerina's started to ease a little. At least now I could put some meaning behind it and not get so lost in it all. Yet deep within, the undercurrent remained and at times those moments of anxiety rose up like a phoenix from the ashes to swallow me whole. There were moments where I thought I would be better off walking away altogether, to turn away and leave it all behind, for that was my pattern, yet my heart insisted otherwise. I began to think what difference would it make now anyway, should this story have any truth? This was a completely different life and even if this did happen, then it cannot be changed. What is done is done. I questioned whether I was going completely mad. I shoved it away into another corner to deal with it another time.

Then unexpectedly, several months later one summer afternoon, I was enjoying a cup of tea with Katerina on her balcony when she mentioned that she had a dream that she wanted to share with me and that maybe I could help her understand it. This took me completely by surprise, as I was the one usually asking for her insight on dreams. What could I possibly have to say that would help? I sat there intrigued as she shared aspects of her dream that aligned with my own Akashic Record reading three months before. She began to tell me the story I knew so well, of the child that I was and whom she loved so much, a young boy that was somehow part of this and the sadness she felt when she had to leave an institution of some kind. That all she wanted was to take me with her but was not allowed; it was forbidden, despite her pleading.

I was stunned speechless and did not know where to even start to try and explain to Katerina my own understanding of this life we had shared. I could barely believe what I was hearing, as the story of her dream unfolded to match the events spoken of in my Akashic Record reading and my experiences at the orphanage, some two hundred years ago. Several hours passed before I could even wrap my tongue around the words to our story. I was in shock and awe at the same time. Firstly, that all that I had been feeling was validated, and secondly, that there was more to our connection than we had ever imagined. To me, her dream provided all the confirmation I needed, and yet at the time I did not realise there was more to uncover still. The orphan child within was about to receive the answers she had died searching for, over two centuries later.

I am sure I am not alone in imagining what it would be like to travel backward and forward in time. In fact, we can, and in turn, bring back pieces of ourselves that have long been missing. Parts of our fractured selves that have fled past traumas and left us feeling incomplete and less whole. That has been my own experience for my entire life; a feeling that something was missing. Even as I married, had children and established a successful career, there was still a space within that could not be filled. I had everything I needed but there was something obviously missing, and yet nothing I could put words to. While my mind would label it as being ungrateful or never satisfied, deep within I knew it to be something more, something perceptible on the fringes yet seemingly unreachable.

Within a few days of uncovering our story and past life connection, I continued to dream about my lifetime in the orphanage. It was as though by knowing this story I now had permission to open up and receive even more, and by doing so I could finally understand all that I still held deep within me on a subconscious level, for both the orphan and my inner child had a deep longing for mothering, a primal need to feel safe, and an overwhelming fear of being left again. The best analogy I can draw on is that described so beautifully by Joan Grant where she states that these two lives could be viewed as "two beads on the same necklace, and the memory they share is contained in the string." For me and my orphan within, not a truer word could be spoken. We could both feel the pull of the motherly love once known and lost, and now within arm's reach, the fear of losing that again was more than either of us could bear. I began to dream more and more of this child, and the young girl's life that was once mine. It was through my dreams that I came to know her name and understand her fears on a level that were comparable to my own.

My dreams of that lifetime were extraordinary, so vivid and detailed that I knew them to be my experience at one point in time. I could feel everything inside the girl's tiny frame, especially the fear behind her eyes and in her heart as she raced against time to find the only mother she knew.

Lottie

My hands are packing snow around a small shrub where we are playing. We are outside, despite the cold, and I am playing a game with the younger children, making them a small house of snow to shelter under. I can see the snow swirling around in front of my face as I scoop more up off the ground. A friend and fellow orphan comes running up to me from behind with great urgency. He whispers in my ear. My heart pitches and rolls in my chest. I drop everything and run in a state of panic. Then, I am suddenly outside my body watching as the young girl runs around the corner of a building, her footsteps leaving prints in the freshly fallen snow. She is thin and pale, her body malnourished, and her long hair is strewn around her face and shoulders. She runs as though her life depends on it and, as if in in slow motion, I watch on from above as I connect with the fear in her eyes. Then, in a second, I am there, back inside her body and looking at the world behind her eyes. I struggle to open them wide, so that I can see. At first, the scenes are blurry, and I think it is just the intensity of the snowfall. Then slowly everything comes into focus and I am running with absolute desperation towards a door I have been to many times before. I know this path well.

  The step at the base of the door is made of stone and worn from a thousand footsteps that have crossed its threshold over the years. I reach out my cold hand and pound on the door, my voice wavering at the thought of what I had just been told. I pound again and shout in a thick Irish accent, "It's me Lottie, please let me in, I beg you?" I know that I can be heard by others and am most likely being watched, but I do not care, all I want is for the door to open, to see her one more time, to see with my own eyes that it cannot possibly be true, that she is still here, that she will never leave me. Surely, she will never leave me. Defiantly I turn the latch, old and heavy in my hands and push the door open. I race into the centre of the room, to see all that I *know is gone. Her bed is perfectly made, and all traces of any personal belongings have been removed. Her room is an empty shell and the woman I love most in the world has vanished. I feel my heart shatter into a thousand pieces inside my chest as I drop to the ground and sob. She has gone, and I have been left behind, again.*

I woke from this dream considerably shaken and upset, my heart was racing, and tears rolled down my face as I struggled to breathe. I rarely cried on waking from dreams, but on that morning, I knew that I had relived something my soul could never possibly forget. It made all the sense in the world and it was in this moment that I was able to understand the feelings that had plagued me for months. I had reconnected with the life of Lottie on yet another level, discovering her name as she pounded on the door, along with the underlying cause of the deep love I felt, and the pain of separation each time I had to leave Katerina behind after a session with her. Deep within, I feared that I would never see her again.

  My dreams of this time continued, and several days later I was woken in the early hours of the morning from a dream hearing a familiar sound, my own tiny footsteps racing down the hall. I knew exactly where I was going and who would be there to welcome me before I even reached the door. The darkness was frightening for a child so young, but I would do anything to be held close while I slept, to feel safe. This feeling of safety and unconditional love from a mother figure was what I longed for, it is what I ached for. I longed to belong. Although Katerina was not my mother in this life, when I was with her she still triggered the same feeling I had experienced lifetimes before, and every part of me remembered this. Even before our past life story rippled to the surface, I had sensed that I had known Katerina before, everything about her felt so familiar and so comfortable yet, I had only known her for several years, but I knew that I loved her with all my heart. This connection we had come to realise, also confirmed the most beautiful, most affirming dream I had in the very early months of our knowing each other. At the time, I dismissed it as ridiculous and brushed it aside, but now I can look back at this and realise what this dream was trying to show me, that we are indeed soul friends and we have known each other for a very long time and have come together in this life for a reason.

Spirit

I am free of bodily form and can see myself as ribbons or streams of golden light moving energetically, spiralling upwards and down, over and over, weaving in and out. I feel the most incredible feeling of peace – yet one that I cannot truly describe with words. It is out of this world and the most beautiful feeling; I feel nothing but absolute love. I am love. I can see another energy form in front of me and we move towards each other quickly to become two streams of light wrapping in and around each other with such joy. We are joining as one in the most beautiful dance and I feel elated and excited at being in the presence of this spirit. We move as one, we think as one and there are no words to describe the feeling of love that flows between us.

I woke suddenly from this dream knowing and feeling in every cell of my body, that the other stream of light was Katerina. I convinced myself that this could not possibly be so, and not to be so ridiculous, that this was just wishful thinking, but my soul knew otherwise, and as such my dreams were trying to guide me gently, so that I could acknowledge my feelings and know that they were valid and real. In hindsight, and from all that has unfolded over the years, I undoubtedly know this to be true. We have come together in this lifetime for a purpose, unknown at the time of the dream, but our relationship was destined to unfold, and is no doubt still unfolding to this day, as our friendship continues to deepen and flourish.

One morning during meditation, and not long after the dream of life at the orphanage, the face of a young girl flashed before my eyes; the same girl I had dreamt of before and seen lying on the cobblestones in the rain. In this moment, the connection became crystal clear and the dream pieces interlocked. I knew she was the orphan Lottie, in her teenage years, whom I hovered over at the moment of her death on that cold winter's night, and that she had died searching for the only mother she had ever known. Physically, she was identical to the same Lottie I saw running around the corner of the building encircled in snow, down to the very clothes she wore. At the time of Lottie's death, so many unanswered questions remained; so much was left unresolved. She did not understand the reasons behind why she had been left so suddenly and, despite her searching, why she had never found her much loved Sister again in that life. There was only one person who could provide these answers for me, and it was only a matter of time before Katerina could explain her reasons for leaving, through the feelings and emotions of who she was in that life, Sister *Maria*. Soul memories had resurfaced for both of us, as we explored this lifetime together in dreams, so that all that had been lost before, could be reclaimed. Ancient wounds were exposed so that they too could be healed.

Lottie is not the only past life I remember through dreams, although it is by far the most detailed and clearest memory I have of a life across time. I can draw on others too, and they are always linked to something that is present in my current life, a thread that ties us together through experience. When I can connect to these memories, I eventually see the pattern, the recurrence of events that enables me to see the bigger picture; the pieces that make up the whole. It is then that I can choose to consciously change my response, or think of a situation in a different way, and to see life's experiences as a gift and an opportunity to learn, whether it be in this life or one that is all but a far memory. From a soul level, it makes no difference, time is irrelevant if there is wisdom to be gained and healing to be done.

As I worked diligently on my issues around the fear of loss and abandonment, I came to learn of another life through a dream that shared this common thread. On this occasion however, I was shown a different ending. It was one that enabled me to see, that despite similar patterns and life experiences, the outcome does not have to be the same, and that we can make a choice to consciously move away from negative expectation and instead perceive an ending that brings joy and peace. This dream provided me with the clarity and wisdom to see things as they truly are and taught me a most valuable lesson in this life, that it is not necessary to live in fear, because life can present the most beautiful surprises, when you are least expecting them.

Rescued

In this life I am a 10-12 year old girl living in Medieval Scotland. I don't receive my name in this dream, but I work in a grand country manor as an agricultural servant. I sense I have no parents or have been abandoned. I am a long way from home or at least the home that I once knew. I work with "Old Tom" who is the senior gardener, and I follow his instruction to the letter. I must not put a foot wrong and so I do what I am told, weeding, harvesting the food and replanting seed under his guidance.

It is a warm summer's day. I am observing the garden from where I stand with its fence made of cut saplings from the nearby forest and tied together with twine. I can see rolling green hills and the stone stables at the rear of the homestead.

The garden is in full bloom and there is much colour in the vines trailing over the garden fence. I feel anxious and am waiting nervously near a gate when I can hear a man's voice shouting at Old Tom, he is telling him in no uncertain terms that I must go, that I no longer have a place here. "Get rid of her," he shouts.

The dream shifts, and I am riding a dapple-grey pony uphill with Old Tom beside me on his white mare. There are two men behind me also on horses, but in time they disappear from the dream. I am nervous, and I fear for my life. I wonder what Old Tom will do to get rid of me, will he take me to the forest and kill me? I am quiet, and all I can hear is the slow, steady rhythm of the horse hoofs beneath me. I am resigned to the fact that I will die, for I have nowhere to go and no one else to take care of me. After some time, we arrive at a house that I have not seen before. It is made of stone and is white washed, built on the side of a steep hill overlooking the valley and moor below. Old Tom brings his mare to a stand and my pony follows her lead. Old Tom turns to me and says, "C'mon Lassie, time to hop off and take a wee rest." I think to myself, "This is where I will die."

I dismount, and I follow Old Tom as he turns the latch on an old wooden door and steps across a worn stone step. We enter a room that appears to be a kitchen and he begins to show me where things are. I am wondering why he is doing this, but I pay attention and listen carefully as I do in the garden. His face softens, and I can see kindness in Old Tom's eyes. He guides me to the rear of the house and we enter a short but dark corridor. He takes me to a room that contains a small bed with a handmade quilt. Old Tom asks me to wait here while he goes to fetch something. I am anxious again, thinking perhaps he will kill me after all, until I see old Tom bring an older woman into the room. She has long grey hair and wears a worn blue dress and a shawl.

I look into her eyes, large and blue like the summer sky, and I can see that she has suffered greatly. I sense that she has lost many children in her life with Old Tom and she is lonely and sad. Her eyes widen and are brimming with tears as she sees me standing before her, as though every dream she has ever wished for has been answered. I know now that I am here to stay, as the child she has longed for and lost over and over again. The dream shifts, and she is by my bed, fixing the quilt and making sure I am warm. I feel safe and I know that everything will be just fine.

When I woke from this dream, it was as though my whole body knew that 'everything will be just fine,' and that the fear of being left and abandoned is just that, a fear, and is one that may not necessarily come true. It was in this dream that the young Scottish girl taught me to believe in miracles and that love and kindness can be found in the most unexpected places, providing me with all that I had ever dreamed of. It was a reminder of all I had found in my relationship with Katerina, and that I had nothing to fear, that everything was exactly as it should be. She was not going anywhere.

Sister Maria

There are many things in this world that can't be readily explained yet feel undeniably true because of our ability to sense intuitively and know when something feels right. Our dreams reveal our inner truth, and it is here on the razor's edge between worlds, that both Kirsten and I received insight into another lifetime we had shared together. How extraordinary that we could both receive distinct details of our lives across time through independent dreams and have the opportunity to share them with each other.

Our dreams as Lottie and Sister Maria provided us with a deep understanding of why we both felt so beautifully connected to each other in this lifetime, for in reality we were experiencing similar emotions we had been through before but had never been resolved. Through our sharing of dreams and experiences from this time, I became reacquainted with Lottie, the sweet orphan child who I had come to love as my own, and my role in her life as Sister Maria, who she loved dearly as the only mother figure in her life. The more dreams we shared, the more space was created for our story to unfold, and my memories from this time became incredibly lucid. During this time of unravelling, I was privileged to receive a series of dreams and insights from meditations that allowed me to connect with our story more deeply and gather the memories that had tied us together then, so that we could set about healing in the now.

Whether in meditation or dreams, these experiences were as real as though I was watching a movie unfold before my eyes, already knowing the setting to be Belfast, Ireland, in the 1700s and during a period of much poverty and despair. As the pieces locked together, so did the story of Sister Maria and Lottie.

Sister Maria

Arriving at the orphanage is my last resort, on a day that is as miserable as I felt, intensified by the dampness and bitter cold. I am heartbroken, as memories surface of my own child of two years, who has been cruelly taken by consumption. Within days of his passing, my grief-stricken pain is doubled with news of the death of my husband, who is a soldier and killed in battle against the French. I feel lost and desperately alone, starvation is rife in the country and life has become unbearably hard. I have come to the end of my road and can see no way out of my predicament.

I see myself walking through the market crowds, where I overhear a conversation between two women talking about an orphanage that desperately needs help. Its walls were stretched to capacity with the sheer number of children who need a roof over their heads and food in their bellies. I realise that this is where I can be of assistance, giving me a sense of purpose and the strength to go on.

I arrive at the orphanage and walk up the front steps to the dark double doors at the entrance, standing tall and foreboding. I stop and pause for a moment sensing trepidation, knowing that my life will never be the same again once I pass across this threshold. I knock three times. Without further ceremony I am ushered into the foyer and asked to wait. It is here that I take the opportunity to look around, only to see a small child with fine brown hair framing her thin face, on her hands and knees scrubbing the floorboards. She barely looks seven years of age. She looks up at me and our eyes connect, her slightly nervous smile striking a cord in my heart.

I suddenly sense a bold and menacing energy to my left and look in that direction to see a man rushing towards me. He is tall with dark eyes and unruly dark hair. His white collar is stained yellow and he wears a black gown that is wrinkled and worn. "Come along, come along," he says as he pushes me into a room. "Sit down" he orders abruptly. I am unsure about his manner, somewhat anxious and suspicious of his demeanour. As he talks he reveals his stained teeth, brown and rotting behind his thin lips. We sit at a table, and he asks me of my business, and so I begin to bravely explain my recent loss, and my need to find somewhere to live and to be of use. As he vehemently lays down the rules, I become aware that the little child who has been scrubbing floors in the entrance, has let herself into the room. Without thought, he points his finger towards the door and screams at her, "Not now!" She picks up her bucket and leaves promptly, and the fear in her wake is palpable.

I feel my whole body respond in disgust at his reaction, and as though reading my mind, he says clearly that under no circumstances must I allow myself to become attached to the children. If that was not possible, then the only alternative is that I must leave, immediately. I know in my heart I have to stay, for it is my only chance of survival in these hard times, but I am also resigned to the fact that there will be much suffering to endure during my time here. Deep in my heart I know that these children need me here, as much as I need them.

The setting shifts rapidly, and I see myself wearing a sister's habit, and that I am to be known as Sister Maria. The orphanage is a harsh environment to live in, and I struggle with the daily abuse of the children, dished out by most of the nuns. Hiding in a dark corner of the hallway my heart feels heavy with sorrow. I stand trembling in the cold, damp environment and my thoughts race towards Lottie. "How can I help this sweet, small innocent child whose sensitive and gentle nature is crushed by the overbearing nuns? How can I create a sanctuary for her, in this place Lottie calls home?" I make the decision, then and there, to discretely reach out to the orphans in any way that I can and provide them with the small things that will make a difference in their lives, actions and words that will go undetected by the nuns I share this home with.

In time it is little Lottie who wins my heart. At night it is my duty to attend the dormitories and make sure all the children are in bed, and the lamps extinguished for the night. I stand at the doorway and cast my eyes over each child, as though giving them a reassuring hug good night with my thoughts alone. Lottie's bed is near the door, and it is here that our eyes frequently connect, where unspoken words and love are received.

One night I dream of my own child in my arms, and I am holding him tenderly. As I look upon him in this dream within a dream, I can see that he is dead. I startle myself awake, to see what I think is a ghost standing by my bed, to suddenly realise it is Lottie. "What are you doing here?" I whisper to her. She stands silently, trembling from the cold that permeates the orphanage. I pull back my blanket and allow her to climb in next to me. She nestles in close and I feel her tiny, frail body next to mine, and her extreme vulnerability. I hold her close all night long as if she is my own, and as dawn approaches, I reluctantly send her back to her room before anyone else awakes. This becomes our pattern, and over time we form a deep and lasting attachment, providing a sense of connection between mother and child; that which is missing from both of our lives.

Years pass, and I can see that Lottie is older, a young girl in her teens. She remains thin and malnourished but has longer hair, and the same eyes I know and love so well. She is particularly fond of taking care of the very young, and I see her caring for them and attending to their needs, giving them all she knows they long for. I sense I am ill during this time and require hospitalisation. I keep this news from Lottie and do not tell her as to spare her the trauma. I only want to protect her, so I slip away quietly, with every intention to return for her when I am *well, and take her with me, but I do not, as I succumb to the illness which takes my life.*

If only I had known then, that it would take me lifetimes to find her again, I would have found a way to tell her my reasons for leaving, and that it was all for love.

Search and Rescue

*"Do not grieve.
Anything you lose comes round in another form."*

RUMI

Sometimes it is possible to return to a point of trauma; that moment in time when your world fell apart, and rewrite history. Of course, it is impossible to rewrite the course of events in one's life, but on another level, at the level of the heart, this CAN be done for greater understanding, acceptance and healing. It has nothing to do with what we think inside our heads, but everything to do with what we feel and how the body experiences this understanding. It is one thing to comprehend something at an intellectual level, but something entirely different when we understand something at a soul level. We *FEEL* it, at the very centre of who we are, and the trauma falls away from us like shedding skin, as too do the conditioned responses we have carried all our life, and perhaps over many lives. It is the most beautiful "Aha" moment.

It was through my dreams, that the loss Lottie had experienced was made known again. But more importantly it was the connection to the emotion of the fear of being left, that led to a deeper understanding. That fear was the impediment to feeling whole, yet ironically it was the path to that fear I needed to take to find trust and security for the child within.

Similarly, for Katerina, it was through the dreams of Sister Maria, that the connection to her feelings of guilt and loss could be made. The anguish of wanting to take a child with her, but not being able to because of circumstances beyond her control. It was here that she could connect the dots and finally express what she had longed to say. How often have we thought, *"If only I could have that time over, I would do things differently?"* We cannot change a past decision or action, but we can change the residual effect of that action, and its hold on the body.

Whether it be Lottie and Sister Maria, me or Katerina, it made no difference in this situation or this relationship, which had sparked from the moment that tiny fissure in my heart was revealed. It set off a chain of events that neither of us were anticipating – links to old memories, shared dreams, deep wounds and forgotten stories. There was only one thing left to do, and that was to rewrite the history that was, and in a way that eased the subconscious emotions each of us was experiencing from that lifetime together. Robert Moss supports this notion in his book *Dreaming the Soul Back Home*, stating that "We want to understand not only how the legacy of past lives may work in our present lives – and may be healed, when seen for what it is – but also how we can reach back across time to heal something in the life of a previous self."

Where do you start? Where it all began of course, at the point of the trauma. For our own story, we were able to revisit the raw emotional space where Lottie was abandoned, and where Sister Maria's heart was broken at having to leave Lottie behind. After the years of work and dreams we had shared together, the starting point for us was not difficult to find, and we could do so easily, being present to support each other. The pathway to these emotions was already there, and we had both travelled it before in dreams. The rewriting of events did not require a great work of fiction, nor did it need script writing finesse, all that was required were just a few words in the safety and comfort of each other's company, "I'm sorry I had to leave. I wish I had told you the truth, but I didn't want you to despair. If I had this time over, I would have been brave enough to tell you." For Lottie, she had the opportunity to say in return "I did not understand, I felt so lost without you, I thought I was to blame, and so I searched and searched for you."

For both of us, these emotions lingered and persisted across time, and were similarly triggered by the events in our current reality. It is true, that we could not pretend or imagine that it happened in any other way, but we could be true to our feelings, both past and present, and honour them in such a way that enabled understanding and resolution. So, it came to be, that the loss for Lottie was acknowledged, understanding was gained and the deep fear that I would be left again dissolved. For Sister Maria, the guilt of leaving Lottie unintentionally was made known, her deepest regrets shared, and the legacy of the past was set free. These emotions that had resided in our bodies for so long bubbled to the surface, filtered through skin and bone, then gradually and slowly disappeared, and have not been seen or felt since. These feelings no longer have a place in our lives, nor need to live and persist into the future. The slate has been cleared and our soul contract with each other fulfilled.

From this moment, we were both free to create any story our hearts desired, and so we have. It is one of understanding and forgiveness, and lasting friendship.

Pink Ted

*"You can't stay in your corner of the Forest
waiting for others to come to you.
You have to go to them sometimes."*

A.A. Milne, Winnie-the-Pooh

I felt so deeply connected to Kirsten I could almost sense when a breakthrough and profound healing was about to occur. In these moments it seemed everything aligned in reality to facilitate the necessary, no matter how small. Looking back on these events, I watched Kirsten continually step forward with courage, to seek and find what she needed to experience wholeness.

During the time I have known Kirsten, I have never doubted for a single moment her ability to know when her inner four-year-old child required attention, the small and fearful child that desperately needed to come home, for too many years had passed without her needs being acknowledged, and the door to her pain had been closed for a very long time. While I sensed much healing had been done, occasionally I would see her rise to the surface, peering through a tiny crack, but the fear often seemed so great for the four-year-old, and the door would be quickly slammed shut again. No one could reach her in these moments, not even her adult self, but I knew she would get there eventually for she was so determined to do so. I simply observed and supported Kirsten during this time, and as she connected to the memories, I began to see many other younger selves emerge from the shadows, as her ten-year-old, fourteen-year-old and young adult self, stepped into the limelight. Her commitment to retrieving her inner child was unwavering. All she needed was time.

A most memorable unfolding occurred early one morning as I was in preparation for my scheduled day. I received a message on my phone from Kirsten early that morning, asking if she could come and lay down for a while on my couch. She said she didn't need anything else, just a quiet space to be, and away from the demands of home and work. I knew in my heart she was facing that door again and there was an inner child knocking for attention.

When I heard her at my front door, I opened it to see her looking pale and forlorn. Without further thought I opened my arms to her and she fell into my embrace, and I held her until she was ready to let go. It was during this time I received a strong image in my mind, that of my grandson's bed in the adjacent room. It was a small portable fold up bed that I used for him when he would come to stay during school holidays, and although he had returned to his interstate home, I had left it in place, freshly made as though I knew it would be needed soon, complete with a small white fluffy polar bear nestled on the pillow.

Without a second thought I led Kirsten to that bed, and pulled back the doona for her to climb in. There, I tucked her in and placed the small bear into her arms which she immediately embraced close to her heart as she cried. She didn't need to tell me what she was feeling or what emotions were surfacing, for I already knew. I drew the blinds and quietly closed the door behind me, for all she needed right now was time and solitude to move through this space gently.

A few days before this visit, during one of our sessions, Kirsten told me that as a child she was very attached to a toy that she could never remember being without, a cuddly bear she affectionately called 'Pink Ted'. He was the one thing that gave her comfort and a feeling of security after her mother left her at the age of four, and she cherished Pink Ted well into her early teen years. She had reached out to Pink Ted every night for as long as she could remember and would put herself to sleep by sucking her thumb and rubbing her nose with Pink Ted's arm. She told me, that over time Ted's arm would wear out and her grandmother would lovingly repair and replace a new covering on Pink Ted's arm with fabric cut from her mother's dressing gown that had been left behind. Although she did not recognise it at such a young age, Kirsten had come to realise that her grandmother knew that the dressing gown provided a connection to feeling her mother close again, and therefore having it stitched to her favourite bear, comforted her as she drifted off to sleep.

The emotional security, support and comfort Pink Ted provided in her life during this time was significant. She and Pink Ted were inseparable. Even at fourteen, Pink Ted was very central to her nightly routine and provided a feeling of security as she slept.

Kirsten continued to tell me that one morning she woke up to find that Pink Ted was no longer there beside her. She thought this strange and became anxious, searching high and low for him, but he could not be found. She had asked everyone in the family if they had seen him, but nobody had. She knew he couldn't just disappear of his own accord, so she thought he would turn up eventually, that perhaps she had put him down somewhere and had simply misplaced him. It was many days later while Kirsten was still searching for her beloved bear, when her older sister told her in frustration that she was wasting her time searching for her Ted; that he had been taken to the incinerator in the back yard and burnt because she was too old for teddy bears and that it was time to let it go.

Kirsten immediately raced to the back yard to where the incinerator was, in hope that he would still be there and that she could perhaps salvage him, give him a wash and he would be as good as new. However, the reality of the moment hit her hard in the chest as she stood on her toes to look inside the incinerator, for all that was left was the darkness of ash and the stench of betrayal. The significance of this loss for Kirsten went unnoticed at the time, but she was heartbroken at the loss of her dearest friend, and deeply traumatised that he was stolen from her arms while she slept. Once again, she had lost something dear to her heart, something she loved so very much, and she was left to relive the trauma of yet another form of abandonment.

As I listened to Kirsten's story, I realised that abandonment, in all its forms, had become a persistent pattern in her life, and the ongoing fear of this was something that she could not seem to shake and was deeply ingrained. Her upbringing in a fragmented family situation was not idyllic for her, and I could see the impact this had caused in her life and the way it fuelled her fear. At the time when the loss of her much-loved bear surfaced, I received a dream that helped me gain my own insight into the depth of her pain, and the deep-rooted responses that were the cause of her anxiety. This dream, while not a reflection of true events in her life, did provide me a glimpse into the world of a step-child, and her longing to belong.

The Step Child

I am observing a new mother and father in awe of their new born son, cooing over him and adoring him, examining every little inch of his tiny body, fresh from the womb; these moments etched in their minds forever. "We must introduce him to the other children," I hear the father say.
"Do we have to?" replied the mother. "Of course, we do!" he exclaimed. "They will be so excited to meet him."

"He's mine," she whispers quietly under her breath.

Three young children enter the room, two of them watch from a distance while the third child shows nothing but intrigue and excitement at her new little brother. "May I hold him?" she asks and is told "Just for a little bit." They place the new born into her arms and she trembles in awe of his smallness, and instantly falls in love with him. But she is only allowed to hold him for 'just a little bit' and in what seems like no time at all, he is plucked from her small arms and is taken away. She watches on eagerly as he has his nappy changed and is fed, then somewhat abruptly she is asked to leave the room. In time she returns and says quietly, "May I hold him please?" Her stepmother replies, "No, not now, maybe later," and deflated she leaves the room once more. She returns again, however this time she seems older and the baby has grown considerably, he can now sit up and play. "May I play with him?" she asks politely.

"Get out from under my feet and stop being a nuisance!"

"But I just want to play with him, he's so cute!"

"Go on, go out of the room, you're taking up too much space!" The young girl could not believe how she is being treated and wonders what she has done wrong. She leaves again, feeling hurt and alone. Nevertheless, she tries once more to enter the room, only to be sent out before she could speak a word. "What have I done, why won't they let me play with my little brother, why don't they love me anymore?" She draws on her courage and decides to go in and give it another try. This time as she enters the room she is followed by a swarm of insects which hover

around her like an aura. As she moves about the room, so do the insects, swarming with intensity until they blacken the walls and ceiling. Her father yells out, "Look what you've let loose!" as he races around the room with fly spray trying to kill the insects, but the more he sprays the greater the mass of insects become. The young girl runs out of the room again, frightened by what she sees.

I woke suddenly from this dream knowing I had dreamt of Kirsten and imagined her as a young child trying to bond with the new baby in her family. I sensed that it was around this time that her stepmother's approach to mothering may have changed, because of her own life changing experience, redirecting her motherly instinct to her new and only child. I could also see that the insects following the child were symbolic of Kirsten's frustration and awkwardness around the new baby, and she carried these insects with her wherever she went, a constant reminder of the rejection she was feeling and the burden of not feeling she belonged anymore.

The father tried his best to get rid of the insects that were following his daughter, symbolic of the worries he had now become plagued with, as he faced the realisation of the dilemma his children were in. That they were left and abandoned once, and now they were experiencing another type of rejection as their stepmother discovered the unconditional love she had for her new born baby. I could sense that he faced the unfortunate predicament of wanting to do what was right for his new wife and child, but without sacrificing the emotional well-being of his own children. A new child in the family was a joyful occasion and one that his new wife had dreamed of, a new family and an enriched life with the birth of her long awaited first child. Through the lens of this dream, I saw that in the ideal world of the stepmother, there was no room for someone else's children.

Laying in my grandson's bed with a teddy in her arms, the young Kirsten seemed lost in the abyss of despair and grief of another significant loss in her life, searching for any way home. I did my best to support her during this phase and I knew it was only a matter of time before she would come through it, but for now, like a mother yearning for the return of her lost child, I waited.

After I had finished with my clients for the morning, I returned upstairs to my kitchen to prepare some soup for her. In time she appeared in the door way and slowly moved towards the lounge to sit down. She had no words for where she had been, and so I offered some soup which she gratefully accepted. As we shared some lunch and as we began talking over a pot of tea, she mentioned that she felt better and a little lighter and I could see that the colour had also returned to her skin. We talked of the trigger for her emotions that surfaced that morning, and the potential reasons as to why she was drawn back in time to that part of her life. I had witnessed her come so far over the years, and I reassured her that this moment was just another layer that required her attention, and she was ready to acknowledge it.

After a while she asked me how I knew what to do - to tuck her into bed and place the teddy bear in her arms, for it was the perfect scenario to help bring her home. She went on to explain quietly at how significant Pink Ted was in her life, and hadn't realised she had held onto his loss for so long. She admitted she felt she was too old to be so precious about a small bear, however she had also come to realise that it was at that age, the age of fourteen, when she decided to bury everything, to shove it all away into a deep corner and seal it shut. This day for her was about acknowledging and accepting her grief and trauma she had experienced at fourteen, when Pink Ted was abruptly and thoughtlessly taken from her without her knowledge. I felt so relieved for her, to have navigated this loss so graciously, and I hoped that she would be able to make peace with this phase of her childhood.

Several days had passed since Kirsten had come to me as the small child longing for the comfort and security of her bear, when I felt something in the air stir and shift. I was at the beach enjoying a swim when I was overcome with an urge to check my phone. I promptly got out of the water to check if there were any messages for me, and not surprisingly a message from Kirsten was waiting, sent just minutes before. I opened it to see an amazing photo of Kirsten's beautiful face, and her freshly shaven head. She had shaved all her hair off! I smiled from ear to ear - transformation complete! What courage she displayed, to retrieve her four and fourteen-year-old from the abyss of abandonment. She had accepted and acknowledged their losses in life, the emotional trauma that she endured at those times, and she was now reborn into a new phase of her life. I was so proud.

To each season comes a time. A time to release the trauma and allow space for emotional freedom. This space is needed for soul alignment, to live authentically with integrity. In the book *Dreaming the Soul Back Home*, Robert Moss describes this process most eloquently in a chapter on Healing. He explains, "Some parts of our soul may have been missing for a very long time...from the time of trauma in early child hood, or in the birth canal, or even inside the womb. We have learnt how dreams will put us on the track of these lost boys and girls, as will a childhood memory. Caring friends, gifted therapists and genuine shamans, can help us to bring them home."

These words describe so beautifully how my own practice has evolved over the years, as I've learnt to recognise the moment in which I'm presented with these lost boys and girls who are waiting to return home. During my thirty years of practice, I've learnt to recognise the abandoned inner child who peers behind the eyes of the adult self. He or she calls out for guidance and for someone to shine a light on the path that leads to home, but it is not always easy. The inner child's trauma can replay like a broken record, reflected as pain in both the mind and body. The onset of these recurring thought patterns results in a sense of separation and aloneness, feeding their vulnerability and emotional pain. These ingrained patterns can inhibit emotional freedom and often perpetuate an inner belief that no one could ever understand, for in fact, they can barely understand it themselves. The concept of 'home' appears unreachable, often not encouraged or understood by the adults in their world, who find it easier to sweep it under the mat, assuming children are unable to understand or that they will adjust in time.

For Kirsten's inner child, even the sight of a mother sharing time with her child was a reminder of all that she did not have, and would never experience in life, and this had kept her grief stricken on a deep emotional level. She did not understand at the age of four as to why she was suddenly without her mother and left behind, and so her inner four-year-old still needed answers to these questions many decades on. Indeed, a mother is consumed with her own feelings arising out of the separation, where the anguish and confusion does not enable her to see the signs that her child is deeply suffering and needs to hear why the security and love of their mother is no longer a constant in their life. Home, the inner home, the place of a child's security, is not the physical home, but the emotional home of a mother's constant presence and love.

My practice as a remedial therapist, combined with my personal experience has finely tuned my sense of awareness in recognising an inner child in need of help. I reach out to these children with the intent to guide them home, simply by giving them the chance to find their child voice, so that they can be heard and acknowledged unconditionally. I reiterate to them that there is no shame in being abandoned or feeling the way they do, for they are not to blame for a decision that they had no part in. In most cases, the adult is not even aware of the wounded child within, until this connection is made. While I have witnessed the heartache of many abandoned and lost children, I have never encountered the story of another mother who chose to leave her children. While it may not be as common, it does happen, but because it is not considered socially acceptable, it is not spoken of or discussed openly. I know only too well how hard it has been myself to say out loud to others, that I am a mother who left her children. These words alone evoke involuntary emotions of guilt and shame, and I see the immediate judgment in the eyes of the listener and how uncomfortable they feel, not knowing what to say.

Mothers in this situation are left feeling very much alone, rejected and ostracised with no one to turn to for support. There is no lonelier world than this, and only adds to the anguish of what a mother is already missing out on; the day-to-day mothering and the little things that you're not there for, reminded through the discussions of friends and acquaintances about their own children. It becomes a constant reminder of the painful decision made to leave, and in many cases such as my own, the choice to leave is made from desperation, never with the intent to harm, but from a place of self-preservation and the will to do what is best for all concerned, especially the children involved.

I did all that I could to make sure my children were well informed of the reasons why I left our family home.

Unfortunately, I have witnessed that this is not the case for most children, and I see how they are emotionally scarred and haunted by not knowing why they were left. Children need an explanation, for so many go on believing that they are somehow to blame, carrying this notion with them into adulthood. The intensity of their unspoken words is palpable, especially when they are not given the chance to say what is on their mind, or in their heart. This simple act of listening and allowing emotion to surface ultimately paves the way, in most cases, for acceptance. It does not matter how old the child is, for I have worked with very mature clients who still need their inner five, six or seven-year-old to have their say. It is a parent's responsibility to talk openly to their children about any separation, and to reassure them over and over, that they are loved, and they are safe. These simple words can be the music in a child's ear, the music that enables them to dance onwards through life.

Transformation

*"I shaved it off, my hair
because I could,
and the accumulating cells were tired of holding on
to sadness and torment
of what never was but could have been.*

*They lie now, somewhere
on this earth
wrapped in plastic, entangled with a million other cells
from other people's stories.*

*How similar they are
but for the shades and tones
that mark their difference."*

Kirsten Leggett

I can still recall so vividly the day I would declare my new-found self to the world. It was a pivotal day for me, one in shedding all that I had outgrown, and a day in acknowledging the woman I had grown to become. At the time, I had no idea what this may look like, all I knew and could feel was that I was ready for it. Everything about it felt new and exciting, yet on reflection, the events that had led me to this point in time had been in the making for decades, unfolding in the most intriguing ways.

I can confidently say, I feel it all began when I was in my early twenties and I was visiting a local outdoor market with a friend when we stumbled across a palm reader. My friend wanted to have a reading with her and begged me to do the same. I was reluctant for I had always feared I would hear something I didn't want to, or that I would be told something that would influence the way I lived my life. However, after her relentless pleading, I gave in and I sat with the woman in her small tent in the sweltering summer heat.

I can still recall how nervously I held my hand in front of hers. I don't recall the finer details of the entire reading all these years later, but I do recall her studying my palm and the words that followed - that one day I would have a near death experience, around the age of forty-six. I remember the sudden stiffening of my body, the sinking feeling in my stomach, and the apprehension I felt as I waited for her explanation. She calmly informed me that I would gain deep insight from this experience, and that my life as I knew it would change, that I would be reborn in a sense. All I can remember at the time, was how relieved I felt that I was still some twenty-five years away from forty-six, and so I promptly put it out of my mind. Buried.

As the years passed by however, and as I approached forty, the memory of that reading still lingered, it was always there fluttering in the background. I would quickly shove it out of the way and bury it again telling myself, "That is five years away, four years away, two years away," and so the years passed until I reached the year that I would turn forty-six.

By this time however, I had been on a deep and transformational journey since Vanessa's passing, and felt as though I was a different person altogether than the woman I was just a few years ago. I looked the same on the outside of course, but on the inside my landscape was vastly different, as I saw life through a new lens, both clear and bright and my heart felt wide open, to everything and everyone. I could see my life from a new perspective, not only of who I really was; my authentic self - but all that I had the potential to be, in this life and beyond. Close friends also commented on how much I had changed, that I even looked different somehow. My immediate family were the most impacted by the change within me and acknowledged the 'new me' as a happier and more contented one.

I recall explaining to a friend one day that I felt as though I could shine a light on every dark corner that lay within. That the memories and events in my life would always be there, but there were no more surprises; I had swept the corners clean. Should these memories arise again, then I knew where they came from and why they were there. I could acknowledge them, observe them and just let them be, without getting wrapped up in the emotion that I was once attached to. When I told her this, she smiled and said softly "That sounds like true freedom to me."

A few weeks after this realisation, I woke up with a sense of adventure running through my veins, and I knew I had to get out of the house, that there was something bigger waiting for me.

The rest of my family was busy doing other things, and I decided I would venture out for a walk on the mountain. I packed what I needed and headed off. I had no idea where I was going to go walking, but simply got into my car and started to drive – I needed to *feel* the freedom I was experiencing on the inside. I was passing through the city when I drove right by a hairdressing salon. Without thinking I pulled over my car at the next available opportunity and said out loud, "I'm cutting off my hair, all of it." I stopped myself for a moment and thought, "Really?" Then heard from somewhere within, an undeniable and strong "YES!" I ventured in to the salon to see if I could make an appointment, but they were fully booked that day.

I got back into my car, thinking that perhaps today was not the right time, and then again, an inner voice nudged me, "Do it today". At that point every part of me knew that if I was going to shave my hair off, then it had to happen today, and the time was NOW. I had grown accustomed to my inner voice and hearing it in this way, for over the past few years it had led me to great insights and had guided me so precisely to exactly where I needed to be on so many levels. I drove into the city, parked my car and walked down the street, calling in to any salon I passed until I found one that could fit me in.

The third salon I entered had a space in an hour and a half, so I made myself an appointment. I filled in the waiting time easily and wandered through town, thought about what I was about to do, the potential reactions I may get, but none of it mattered, I needed to do this for myself and no one else. I felt so light, as though I was literally about to disappear. I had done a lot of cutting away and shedding of old stuff over the past few years, but this was the ultimate shedding, and felt as though it was the last bit of my old self that needed to go.

    Needless to say, when I returned to the salon for my appointment, the young hairdresser could hardly believe my request when I asked her to shave off my hair. "But you have a really nice hair style," she exclaimed, and it took her at least five minutes to put the clippers to my head, asking repeatedly if I was sure I wanted to do this. I had never been surer than in that moment, and as the last of my hair fell to the floor, I looked into the mirror and saw myself as the woman I had grown to become. I ran my hands over my freshly shaven head and thanked her. I remember her saying how much it suited me, and then asked me how I felt. "Like a new person," I replied. I left, and I walked down the street with the autumn sun warm on my back. I felt the cool air on my freshly shaven scalp and I had never felt more alive than in this moment. I had arrived!

    In a meditation several weeks later, I came to the sudden realisation that this was my near-death experience, referred to in my palm reading all those years ago. In fact, I had been dying a slow death for the past few years, slowly acknowledging and letting go aspects of my former self that had kept the real me from shining through. The prediction of a near death experience was not one associated with my physical body, but that of who I once was. It was the death of old patterns and conditioning, and the emergence of the new me. I was ripping off the mask. This realisation, brought with it memories of a dream I had in the days leading up to shaving off my hair – a prediction of the physical transformation that was about to take place, and my guide for the journey, the Salamander.

Transformation

I am in the forest playing a game with a young girl. She is no more than five or six years of age. We are laughing and having a lot of fun. There is a soft light that shines through the forest canopy and bathes the forest floor in a golden hue. As I am playfully holding on to the girl, I accidentally pull at her clothing a little hard and one of her daisy buttons pops off and lands on the forest floor. She laughs at me, and I tell her to go on while I search for the button, and that I will catch up with her soon. She does so, quite happily, and I go down on my hands and knees and start searching for her button.

I am looking everywhere and wonder why I cannot see something that should be so obvious amongst the leaf litter. I brush my hands over leaves and twigs, and still it is nowhere to be seen. I stand up to gain a better view, and it is at this point that I see the earth begin to move. I step back and watch the earth ripple like a wave until I see a large snout start to emerge from the ground underneath. At first, I think "A lizard?" but as one limb surfaces followed by another, I realise it is a giant salamander emerging from the depths of the earth. Once it has its two front limbs out of the ground, it slides forward to land at my feet. It is twice the size of me and coloured amber with brown spots over various parts of its body. It opens its eyes, glances in my direction, and moves into a patch of sunlight on the forest path. I observe it quietly, awestruck by its presence.

I had never recalled dreaming of a salamander before until this moment, and like other dreams with significant meaning, I could recall the finest of details and woke with the familiar tingling sensation all over my body. I remember it being exceptionally early in the morning, but I got up anyway knowing I needed to find out more about the salamander and why it had appeared in my dream. I searched online for further insight into this animal, its behavioural characteristics and whether there was indeed any dream symbolism for this particular creature. I was aware of this animal, although not native to my home, and for me a salamander seemed the most unlikely creature that would appear in people's dreams. To my surprise however, the first description I found provided me with the answer I was looking for.

    The article suggested that salamanders are perhaps one of the stranger creatures to appear in dreams, and that their presence requires careful contemplation, for these creatures are nothing if not ambiguous. It went on to explain that some have patterns on their skin, as did the salamander in my dream, and that this feature reinforces their mystical element; elevated beyond the physical into the realm of mythology and legend. As such, to dream of a salamander, can indicate a profound symbol of transformation, as it represents being consumed by the creative fire, but not being destroyed by it. When a salamander appears in a dream, it may indicate that this process of being consumed, is one that will not end life, but reinvigorate it. Somewhat like a phoenix rising from the ashes I thought. The article explained that a salamander often appears in dreams at importantly creative junctures of one's life. That the transformative fire associated with this creature, had a deep spiritual association and may indicate the entering a new phase of spiritual development, often after a period of great suffering.

Being a primitive creature, the salamander can symbolise that which rises from the deepest, darkest areas of the psyche, and often during a period of seeking or deep reflection. On reading this interpretation, there was no mistaking the significance of this dream and that indeed this time in my life was pivotal on many levels.

On the night following the salamander dream, I had another, which I felt was clearly linked to the overlying message of transformation. The reason I knew it was linked, is due to the setting and tone of the dream, where I found myself on the same path and in the same forest where I encountered the young girl and the salamander. This time however, I was on my way to my Aunt's house deep in the forest.

The Funeral

I walk along the same path that the salamander had laid on in the patch of sunlight, until I arrive at the front door of my Aunt's forest home. I knock on the door, anxious to go inside as it is getting dark. I knock and knock and am starting to think that no one is home, when I hear noises on the other side. My Aunt greets me at the door and welcomes me in. She seems upset by something, sad almost and I ask her if she is okay. She thanks me, gives me a hug and simply replies, "I'm just glad that funeral is over".

I woke abruptly, thinking, "Whose funeral"? It was not until many weeks later that I realised the funeral referred to in my dream, was mine. It was the funeral for my old self, and the shedding of my hair represented the final stage in the journey of my 'old' life. It was the final act. Curtains. My dreams were a confirmation of the transformation that had occurred, and the twenty-five-year-old prediction of a near death experience, through the cutting away of old attachments and all that tied me to the pain. For many years I had wondered whether the near-death experience, once predicted in a reading, would manifest. It did, but not in the way I had expected.

With this experience I have come to realise that with death of any kind, there is always a new beginning. We only have to look around us in nature to see this happening every day. As the majestic tree falls to the earth from old age, its seeds stored in the soil beneath its roots will sprout and grow to become present again, just as the moon and sun both fall, only to rise again each day. Death is part of life, and opportunities for new beginnings present themselves to us when we are ready for them, whether it is establishing a new way of life after the passing of a friend, or shedding the shackles that have kept us restricted from being who we really are.

It is our way home to Love.

Full Circle

<u>*Katerina*</u>

The moment Kirsten walked through my practice door, I knew there was something more to her than I could see on the surface. I couldn't articulate what that was at the time, but I was intrigued from the outset. It was as though I felt the shift before it arrived, like one anticipates the colours of dawn, or the beauty of a rising full moon on the horizon. I never knew at the time how important her presence would be in my life, or indeed how much she would teach me along the way. What a gift it is to find an old friend, spiritual daughter and teacher all rolled into one beautiful human being.

    My intuition on the significance of our meeting was realised when Kirsten first revealed her inner four-year-old and her story of abandonment, and it was here that I connected with my guilt and shame at leaving my own children, not realising the hold it still had on me decades on. I struggled with the conflict of wanting to assist Kirsten in the way she needed, and the feeling that somehow, I was involved in her pain by playing the role of the perpetrator, and that she would see me in this light if she knew what I had done. I felt it would be the ultimate betrayal to continue to help her in this way, and so I owed it to Kirsten to tell her my story – the truth and as the mirror to her own experience of abandonment. I dearly wanted to support her, for I knew I could help her move through this in time, and for me, would go some way in compensating for the pain I felt I inflicted on my own children.

It was my expectation that Kirsten would walk away once she knew the truth, and would want nothing more to do with me, for how could it be any other way for her, to be faced with the root cause of her trauma. I was surprised and somewhat relieved that she accepted and embraced my story with kindness and understanding. It was at this point, that I could clearly see how worthy this relationship could be and the many benefits that could be gained by facing each other's stories. By all accounts, it appeared that we were both ready for this.

When it came to write this chapter and what it means to come 'full circle,' I needed to deeply enquire and explore what this really means for me. I could certainly look back and observe the patterns in my life, the cause and effect of my decisions, the lessons I had learnt, yet there still seemed to be something missing. My story felt at a loose end and it bothered me, so one night before sleep, I set the intention for a dream that would show me what I needed to see. It is no surprise that my question was answered in a brief and powerful dream.

Who is Judging Who?

I am standing in a court room wearing a crown on my head before a high court judge. She is sitting behind the bench in her dark gown, sporting a white wig on her head as they do in the old English tradition. Looking at me curiously she asks, "What is that you have there?"

"A box," I reply.

"Bring the box to me!" she demands, and I place it on the bench while she examines the outside of the box, then promptly asks me to open it. I remove the lid, and inside, to her surprise and mine, is a head!

"Who judged this person?" she asks.

"I did," I reply.

"To whom does this head belong?" she asks again.

"It is I, I am this head. I judged myself. I did what I had to do, then I judged myself!"

Waking abruptly from this dream, its meaning was immediately clear to me. I threw off my bed covers and went straight to the window, pulling the curtains aside and letting the morning sun shine into my bedroom, feeling the sun's rays shining brilliantly on my heart centre. My thoughts immediately returned to a place that had been long hidden, the place where the fissure lay embedded in my heart, triggered by Kirsten's inner four-year-old child. I knew its origins only too well. It had formed the moment I gave my answer to the father of my children, the moment I reluctantly decided to give him the answer he wanted most. It was the hardest moment of my life, to form and say the words, "Yes, you may have the children."

At that time, I could hardly believe my own mouth, that these words were coming from me, and as I stood there in my bedroom with the sun beaming onto my chest, I sank into the memory, my entire world turning black as though the darkest cloud had swallowed me whole. I tried so hard to keep it together until they drove swiftly away, my three little angels in his charge, he, completely oblivious to the shattering of my heart that pierced my soul. Life was never to be the same for any of us again. This was my 'ground zero' and from that moment on, as I pushed my shame into my subconscious, so did I also change the trajectory of my health, as the underlying impact began simmering away within the marrow of my bones; the consequence of the decision I had made.

Ideally, this could have been my defining moment, the point in time when a new life could have unfolded, a chance to evolve in my own way and live a life on my terms. But I hadn't accounted for the backlash of the psychological conditioning of my formative years which promptly held me captive in my own personal prison. I could now see the pattern and that it was 'I' that I wished to get away from, for it was with 'I' that the issue persisted, not with anyone else. I did what I had to do to free myself, but then I judged myself, and cut off my head.

It was here, at this point that a part of my soul was lost for I couldn't bear to live with the consequences of my decision.

I could not prevent this happening, nor could I foresee it, and it was then that the weight of self-deprecation, self-judgement, anger, resent, guilt and shame, had fallen upon me like chains around my ankles, preventing me from stepping forward into a future I had longed for. I had been held prisoner by my intolerable grief, and the loss of my children had me bound in my own anxiety, guilt and shame. Although they were with me on weekends and holidays, the time between seeing them seemed eternal, and with each visit there was always an adjustment period as they settled in with me. It took time for us to be comfortable together. I could blame only myself for this because I had inflicted this upon myself. It was all 'I'.

In this moment of realisation, on that sunny morning in my bedroom, I dropped into the foetal position on the floor and began to sob, my head on my knees, my face streaming with tears. I felt my emotions from this time rising, slowly building up to a toxic crescendo of bellowing cries, like prisoners of old, locked up in confinement for years on end and then one day set free. The door to the cell is open and I am exposed to the light. I am the prisoner crying out in pain, as the sun's rays pierced and burned my new seeing eyes.

The fear of freedom was overwhelming, as my self-confinement over the years had caused me an unnatural fear of the freedom I so desperately yearned for. I could not recall what it was like to feel this free. The truth is, although I had long dreamt of it, I had never really experienced it until this moment, and it was here that I recognised the trade-off; that in finding freedom, I had also shattered that which I'd valued most in my life. Freedom, it seemed, had come at a great cost, and I wasn't even sure it had provided me with the answer I was searching for. Emotions of disdain, resent, anger, self-loathing, shame and guilt had been simmering in my bone marrow all these years.

Some time passed as I gradually emerged from this deep, dark and cathartic place. Then gradually a lightness gently washed over me as I felt celestial angels spiralling around my body, taking with them the suffering and deep emotional pain from my entire being, enveloping me in love. I felt a deep cleansing of my soul had just occurred, my heart now light, open like never before and ready to receive again. Ready to receive the love I once felt I didn't deserve. The cup had been emptied, and I knew that now it must be filled with self-love.

As I recovered from this moment, I still felt something remained unfinished, and there was more that I needed to acknowledge. I meditated on this notion briefly and the answer came like a lightning bolt. I needed to return to the place of 'ground zero' and so with a few deep, long breaths I returned to the moment in time when I chose to leave, except on this occasion I faced my husband with such clarity, and with the strength of the person I am today. Only months ago, I had decided to create my version of a parallel life, to revisit the moment of leaving and choose a different outcome, by taking the children with me. Yet in this moment of even greater clarity, that outcome didn't feel right either, as though all it was doing was creating a bypass to something I needed to experience. Seeing myself leave with the children was not the answer my soul was seeking, because in reality it did not happen that way. It was not the truth. I knew in my heart that I needed to make peace with the fact that I let him have the children and that I needed to make peace with my "yes" answer, that he could take our children with him. I knew my body needed to feel okay with this.

I closed my eyes to look directly into his and to connect with him at a soul level. The feelings from that time in my life rose quickly, my gut still churning and head swimming as though this memory was from yesterday. I called out for courage to find my voice, to speak the truth as it was, and like a lion's roar my voice rose, and the words came flooding out. "Yes, yes! You can take the children with my blessing. It's okay." My heart was calm with resolve and in this stillness a sense of peace, like I had never known, gently flowed from my heart, and with it I embraced us both. It was in this moment that I felt we had finally sealed our karmic contract with each other, the contract we had made for our greatest learning. I visualised my children who were sitting quietly in the car, and as peace continued flowing I spoke gently, "My darlings, I love you all, more than you will ever know. However, I need to let you go and live with your father in his care, safely in your beautiful home." I held each of them in my arms and with all my heart told them that I would forever be in their lives and love them dearly. They are part of me, my three peas in a pod. I blessed them, holding them individually in my arms, squeezing them with all my heart until we merged as one, then released them gently. I stood silently and watched as the car drove away and vanished from my sight.

In this state of acute awareness, I imagined the brilliant light within my heart expanding as I continued to give thanks with all my heart and soul to everyone who had walked with me on this path, and for the lessons they had provided along the way. I observed this beautiful light expanding from their hearts back to mine. I felt I had just turned a monumental corner in my life and was the turning point in releasing the shackles I had created for myself over the years. In this last hour I had learned so much about myself. The lightness and peace within me continued to expand as far as it could reach, into the Cosmos.

I gave thanks and gratitude to the Giver of Life, God, the Field, the Universe, whatever it is you'd like to call it. Let it be Spirit! In this moment I could sense a cosmic connection of Oneness with all Existence. It is difficult to find words for such a humbling moment, but I felt nothing but connection with everything on this beautiful planet governed by nature, our Mother of All, Gaia, providing all that we need, and the realisation that it is love that holds it all together. We are of one Mind, one Heart, one Spirit, and we cannot do something in life without causing a ripple effect for all concerned. As the Chaos Theory rings true, "something as small as the flutter of a butterfly's wings, can ultimately cause a hurricane across the other side of the world." I have learnt to be ever present with my thoughts, knowing that thoughts are things. If you think it or perceive it, then so it shall be. Life choices need to be made with the deepest sense of consideration, and ultimately no one on this earth will ever judge you harder than yourself.

Finally, I realised that there was one more thing I needed to do, and that was to forgive myself. Imagining my form in front of me, I observed a brilliant light and divine love penetrate my own heart, flooding my whole being to the core with love. Only now was I ready to take my head from the judge, retrieve it from the box, and put it back on.

It was Kirsten's vulnerable inner child who opened my eyes and heart, as she spoke those haunting words in my office that day, "My mother left me when I was four," cutting deep and ripping my heart wide open, exposing all I had been in denial of. The light that was let in chased away the shadows that obscured my truth, allowing me to finally face my Self! Giving thanks to Kirsten does not seem enough, for a gift as precious as this, is surely a gift from God. The courage and vulnerability of her four-year-old abandoned child within saved me, and while she came to me seeking healing, ironically it was she who aided my healing also. I have no doubt we were meant to come together in this life for so many reasons; to nurture and cherish an extraordinary 'Soul-ship' and find within it my soul daughter.

It is only now that I feel I have come full circle on this path and I am excited about the future and the joy it holds. I feel I have retrieved my heart in fullness, and a part of my soul that had long been missing. No longer do I feel dominated by feelings associated with a lack of self-worth but see an open road ahead with dreams to explore and a life to be cherished.

Through my own life experiences, I have learnt how our mind, body and soul are inseparable for if I am stuck in one, I am stuck in all. Our stories remain entrenched within us at a cellular level, until such time we realise that to find peace within ourselves, within our heart and soul, we need resolution. Otherwise we remain fragmented, continually searching for the parts of our soul that are missing. We must learn to listen to our heart, pay attention to our dreams and intuition, quieten our minds to allow the voice of our soul to be heard. It is here we can find a treasure trove of answers that lead to healing and becoming whole again. It is the path to self-love.

Kirsten

I did not go looking for this journey of self-discovery, for it found me in the most unexpected way. Grief, I can say was the starting point. I read once that, "In order to heal it you need to feel it". That much I know is true. For me, to do that I needed to dive right in to the memories and transport myself back in time. I could never have imagined just how far back I would journey, but in doing so, I know that there is more beneath the surface than we realise, and that our fears, anxieties and behavioural patterns can stay with us – even between lives and across time. When we can acknowledge these patterns and the triggers that cause us to react, we can observe them for what they are and where they have come from, and in doing so we have the ability to change our reaction to these triggers, and find a new path forward, void of old patterns and conditioning. I think of it as pulling a loose thread, and instead of it getting snagged on old ways, it is free to fly on the wind.

It took over forty years for me to realise that I was not whole, and the 'missing' part I had always felt was in fact real, and not just some superficial and selfish need to have more. It was far from superficial, but embedded in every cell, every breath I had taken since the day my mother left me behind and walked out the door of our family home. The irony of it all, is that my inner four-year-old had no way of finding a way out of this place on her own. She could only be retrieved by a loving mother who cared enough to reach out her hand, extend it down the darkest of holes and search for her, relentlessly, because she too wanted her home and back close to her heart where she belonged. This is where the true healing began, for no matter how difficult it became or how hard it was to face the emotion that surfaced, I was never given up on, never turned away, never left again to suffer in four-year-old silence. This is what I call, and feel blessed to experience, a journey of great love.

To come full circle meant I needed to return to the point of trauma, to meet my inner four-year-old and integrate her into the spirit of my adult self. This, after all, was what I was being called to do – to acknowledge and listen to the child within, allow her to find her voice and eventually her way home to wholeness. I knew when my work was done, for not only did I feel and look like a different person, but a dream also acknowledged that the hard work was over. I had done all that was required and had fulfilled my promise to honour and retrieve my inner four-year-old child.

Contract Fulfilled

I am visiting a house that is somewhat familiar. It is a typical beach house but perched high on a cliff overlooking the ocean. I walk up towards the front door and notice the white picket fence out the front. I push gently through the white gate attached to it and walk up the garden path onto the veranda. I notice the colourful flowers either side of the path, and I absorb the serenity of this moment, the stillness in the air and the warm sunshine on my face.

The front door is wide open, and I can see through to the front of the house and out to the ocean, which is shining bright in the intense sunshine, sparkling like a sheet of diamonds. The light within the house is so bright from the sun and the walls are a brilliant white. I call out, for I know someone is waiting for me here, they are expecting me. "Hello, I'm here," I call out. I wait and there is no answer, but I hear a noise from inside and so I let myself in and walk into the front room, but still I find no one here. I can hear the waves below on the shore, but otherwise all is quiet. I hear the noise again, and I move towards the room that the sound is coming from. "Hello?" I say again, quite calmly, and as I walk through the second door I see the back of a man who disappears through yet another door. "Oh, there you are," I think to myself and follow him. He is leading me deeper into the house room by room.

I enter through a third door to see the back of the man standing in the middle of the room. I recognise him from behind, as though he is an old friend, and a highly respected one. It is an honour to be in his company. He is standing still and looking out a large window to the ocean. I say again, "Hello, I'm here." I walk up closer to stand directly behind him, and as I do so, he turns to face me. I look at his face, but he has no face at all, instead all I can see is a faint outline of his head, somewhat like an aura, and the space where his face would be, is filled with an intense and luminous white light.

The light shines out brilliantly and engulfs my whole body. I am so surprised by this, and so I look closer to see where the light is coming from. In the depths of his white light, I see the outline of a human face forming, as though it is appearing from a long way away. First the outline of a nose, then brow and cheekbones. The formations of his face move forward so that I can see it more clearly– an acknowledgement of features that were once familiar to me. He is reassuring me that we are known to each other. I relax, and as quickly as I do, the features disappear again into the brilliant light. I no longer see 'him' for all that is left in this room is the light that shone from his centre, and it both surrounds and fills me completely.

I am standing in the midst of a brilliant and powerful light and I feel it in every cell of my body. I am slowly pulled from this dream, in total awe and feel that he is no longer in my presence, that I no longer need him to guide me in the way that he has. Our work is done, and it is time for me to 'leave the nest.'

I was completely awestruck by this dream, and so grateful to receive this acknowledgement from spirit. Even though there was not a single word spoken between us, I emerged from this dream with an inner knowing that I had been deeply rewarded for my persistence, and not turning away from a four-year-old girl who desperately needed me and knew that I could take great care of her. To arrive at this point did not come easily, and did require surgery of sorts, of the mind and soul, using tools of keen observation, patience, acknowledgement and ultimately acceptance. It required dedication, determination, unwavering courage and the will for emotional freedom.

Most importantly, it was made possible through the demonstration of deep compassion from Katerina who so desperately wanted to understand, and to do so, was willing to step into those ill-fitting shoes one more time. I know I could not have achieved all that I have without her. Together on this journey we created a different and brighter future by reshaping our understanding of the past and the trauma we both experienced. I believe, and always will, that our meeting was not by chance, but guided by dreams, intuition and a deep connection to soul. Our timing could not have been more perfect.

Through this deep and spiritual connection, my four-year-old has found the safety in which to express herself, my ten-year-old has learnt that circumstances in life are just that, circumstances, and she is not to blame. My fourteen-year-old has found the courage to trust again, and my twenty-two-year-old has found the solace she was searching for in a mother. Most importantly, all past, present and future versions of myself have discovered the true and beautiful meaning of what it means to experience the mothering I longed for. In my heart and soul, that is all that matters.

Bibliography

[i] O'Donohue, J., 1997, *Anam Cara, A Book of Celtic Wisdom*, Harper Perrenial, reprinted in 2004, New York.

[ii] Kirsten Leggett, *The Orange Space*, Peregrine Publishing, April 2016, p85.

[iii] David Whyte, 2015, *Consolations. The Solace, Nourishment and Underlying Meaning of Everyday Words*, Many Rivers Press, USA, 2015, p.101.

[iv] Moss, Robert (2012), *Dreaming the Soul Back Home*, New World Library, Novato, CA.

[v] Tick, Edward, *The Practice of Dream Healing*, 2001, Quest Books Theosophical Publishing House, pp 30-31.

[vi] Clarissa Pinkola Estes, *Women Who Run With the Wolves*, 1992, Rider Publishing, pp.23-27.

[vii] Edgar Cayce's A.R.E. *Akashic Records, "The Book of Life"*, http://www.edgarcayce.org/

[viii] Reimers, M. *Akashic Record Reading*, Website http://akashicrecordreading.org/

[ix] Joan Grant, 1956, *Far Memory*, reprint, retypeset edition, 2009, Dawn Chorus Press, USA.

www.ingramcontent.com/pod-product-compliance
Lightning Source LLC
Chambersburg PA
CBHW071912290426
44110CB00013B/1357